Two plays

Soul of Kansa and Kokua

Two plays

Soul of Kansa and Kokua

Bijoy Kumar Satapathy

Translated by
Sanjeet Kumar Das

BLACK EAGLE BOOKS
Dublin, USA | Bhubaneswar, India

 Black Eagle Books
USA address:
7464 Wisdom Lane
Dublin, OH 43016

India address:
E/312, Trident Galaxy, Kalinga Nagar,
Bhubaneswar-751003, Odisha, India

E-mail: info@blackeaglebooks.org
Website: www.blackeaglebooks.org

First International Edition Published by
Black Eagle Books, 2024

SOUL OF KANSA AND KOKUA
by **Bijoy Kumar Satapathy**

Translated by **Sanjeet Kumar Das**

Original Copyright © Bijoy Kumar Satapathy
Translation Copyright © Sanjeet Kumar Das

All rights reserved. No part of this publication may be reproduced, stored in a retrieval system, or transmitted, in any form or by any means, electronic, mechanical, photocopying, recording or otherwise without the prior permission of the publisher.

Cover & Interior Design: Ezy's Publication

ISBN- 978-1-64560-506-5 (Paperback)
Library of Congress Control Number: 2024930959

Printed in the United States of America

For
Swopna, my daughter
Sujata, my wife
and
Bapa and Maa

Author's View

If we don't analyze mythical characters with the yardsticks of modernity and adjust ourselves to their modified sense of values, they will reach a saturation stage, and there will be no more growth. It seems to me that their greatness and significance will be blighted somewhere in the history of the nation.

Kansara Atma was scripted in 1976 and staged in 1980. I have considered the image of Kansa as the soul of Kansa in this play. He symbolizes injustice, exploitation and oppression spread in the society. He resides very much in an individual's mind. Many revolutions and the stream of social evolution or reformation couldn't destroy it or can't beat it. It may be enshrined in history that the revolution of the ruled sometimes dethroned the autocratic ruler, or the ruler was defeated cruelly. A new system of governance is observed in the society, but everywhere, Kansa remains unaltered. His movement is worldwide. He has mingled himself very much with the atomic and subatomic particles. Krushna and other great persons who have descended on earth are unable to take any appropriate action against him. The play, comprising two acts, sheds light upon two different governance systems and the power dynamics of the social structure. The play is without any female characters. There is no need for such characters in the play. One actor can play two roles in the drama. In Act-I, the characters like Andhak, Chaturaksha, Bayasya, Rakshi, Satyabrata, Dharmapal, Councilor-II and in Act-II, the characters Andhalochan, Chaturasen, Manager, Constable, Satyabrata, Dharmapal, Police Officer and the Factory Workers will perform on stage.

On the whole, eight persons will act in sixteen roles in it. In Act II, like other characters, there is no change in the names of Dharmapal and Satyabrata. The people have been like them for ages. The revolution against injustice only succeeds positively many times. Sometimes, the voice can be suppressed. The two acts of the play reflect this. The amateur theatre group 'Prateek' staged the play *Kansara Atma* successfully at the field of Banapur High School on 05 April 1980. For this, I am grateful to the secretary of the institute, Sri Banmali Chualasingh, and other organization workers. I will also thank the Tahasildar of Banapur Sri Pitambar Jena for his valuable suggestions in producing the play. Besides this, the lecturer of the Department of Psychology, Sri Umacharan Das, the lecturer of the Department of Physics, Sri Jitendra Prasad Ray, my bosom friend Niranjan Nayak, and painter Rabi Maharana are equally responsible for its success. At last, I want to convey my gratitude to the lecturer, Dr. Suresh Pattanayak.

Bijoy Kumar Satapathy
Shulia, Kalan,
Dharmashala, Cuttack

Prologue

(From a viewer's pen)

Play is a visual art. A play may be highly intellectual in its theme, but it should be presentable on stage. Of course, the staging of the play is a team effort. Still, the success of the play depends upon the playwright. The playwright is responsible for the selection of theme, characterization, script development, segregation of scenes, and, after all, the uninterrupted inner flow of the play. The story may need to be stronger in terms of modernity, but with a strong character, the play will be readable and presentable on stage. In today's world, most playwrights argue that the success of the play depends on a particular group of audience/ viewers. They are also right to some extent, but like modern poetry, contemporary drama should not be untouched. One person reads poetry, whereas many people watch and enjoy the different aspects of drama simultaneously.

Considering the points above, the success of the play *Kansara Atma* of Bijoy Kumar Satapathy may be discussed. The *Kansara Atma* is called a short experimental play. The soul of Kansa is the soul or the essence of this play. The two acts of the play are in two different environments- one is the imaginary background of the royal court, and the other is the modern estate of an industrialist. The foodstuff of this play is the injustice and oppression of the self-centric influential people against the poor, the distressed and the oppressed, and the revolution against this power dynamics of the contemporary society. It highlights the concept of 'Class Conflict'. The play starts after the announcement of the stage manager. Kansa comes to the stage. Kansa has announced that he will govern as a representative of the oppressive ruling system or a tyrant for ages. The playwright has used the potent myth of Kansa as a new technique in this play.

The dialogues of Kansa are compelling, and the Kansa character has generated a mixed feeling of terror and wonder in the people's minds. Every viewer was mesmerized or hypnotized while watching the play. In Act-I of the play, the king and his team of councillors will present themselves like the characters of a historical or a mythological play in terms of dress code, dialogues and acting for the audience's enjoyment, and the earnest effort and the intellect of the playwright to exhibit the soul of Kansa in the character of the oppressor Andhak. Like the mythological Kansa, King Andhak exploits Satyabrata and Dharmapala excessively. His advocacy is to annihilate the opponents who stand against him bravely. This symbolic representation, on the whole, creates a revolutionary temperament in the audience's minds. Like Act I, the stage manager also comes to the stage before Act II starts and hints at the soul of Kansa changing different bodily form through another character from the mythological age to the Contemporary Period. After the departure of the stage manager, Kansa presents himself again on the stage and announces the rebirth of his invincible and immortal soul—

this intellectual element of Act-I is well-substantiated here. The playwright is successful enough to draw the attention of the people. Here, the elements of traditional opera work out as a carrier of thoughts for the play appropriately.

All the characters of Act I do present and act in different roles in Act II. The play's theme suddenly shifts from the old traditional background to the modern society. As an industrialist, the viewers watch the King Andhalochan in Act I. The oppression and exploitation of the factory owner upon the workers and the government officials who receive extortion and their undue assistance to this industrialist is the central message of Act II. Within the limited boundary of this act, the playwright has briefly and tactfully cited different illegal practices of the contemporary world. From the age of Myth to the modern era, the lawless, corrupted, oppressive rulers position themselves at every step of society to exploit the ordinary people because of their wealth and power, and when the general public takes rest for a while, after exterminating the vast Empire of lawlessness and anarchy, another illegal empire crops up powerfully for the audience to feel. This is what reflected beautifully in the play *Kansara Atma*. Kansa of the mythological age, Andhaka of the historical age, and Andhalochan of the modern democratic country represent the class of corrupt rulers and officials. Based on their ages, there may be differences in their names and dress codes, but in work, they are not different. In every age, the ordinary people, having revolted against the social system, become weak but can't destroy the soul of Kansa; so, for all ages, the playwright has made the people aware of the surroundings.

Though the playwright has kept himself away from the earlier play tradition, he has mastered his voice by juxtaposing the two different backgrounds for a new way of streaming his thoughts. The people have watched the ghastly uncanny form of tyranny by the entry of Kansa on stage. The viewers can't realize the importance of the female protagonists in the play. This is also another victory for the playwright. Moreover, the play is experimental but not unintelligible to the audience.

The playwright Bijoy Kumar Satapathy, is a new promise to the field of modern Odia plays. Like his *Phasilara Nidradrabhanga* and *Bibarna Sahara, Kansara Atma* is also not confined to any particular time, or place or person. The essence of the play is acceptable and intelligible to the audience.

Prof. Suresh Pattanayak

Translator's View

Man lives in the community. When his heart is full of love, compassion, and justice, and he thinks of others for a healthy and sound society, he earns respect everywhere. Trapped in doubt, disbelief and scepticism, if he propagates the message of 'terror and menace' in the community, he is symbolically regarded as an evil spirit. Because of his rationalistic thoughts, in this modern age he has travelled a lot in the field of science and distances himself away from humanism and spiritualism. He focuses on industrial growth and prosperity to hoard more and more and stays firm in the cut-throat competition. Anarchy is galvanized everywhere. Nobody rests peacefully. Disappointed in the social system, the ordinary people earnestly invoke God to incarnate or to descend in any form or send somebody as a messiah to protect the world that has already been created by Him and is now diseased. In other words, there is a need for social reformation or transformation. The pangs of woes and agonies the people suffer from pave the way for the rise of movements against the established social tradition. A new system comes into power, replacing the erstwhile one, but the suffering of the ordinary people never ends. The poor and the wretched are the root cause of any change. Once they come forward to join the social movement, a sea-change is inevitable and perceived.

There is no nexus between the poor and the rich. The rich become richer, and the poor become poorer. The suffering of the poor never ends. The aboriginals and the marginalized ones of society lose their faith in the system that is predominantly regulated by the bourgeoisie class. The classless society becomes a utopian concept. The voiceless groups need to be empowered. The social system is mired inclusively around controversies, discrimination, disparity, and oppression. The unconstitutional practices could be shaken and uprooted, if we developed ourselves psychically and socially. All individuals are to put their heads together for the development of society and the world, plunging into the network of alignment systems. Staying together peacefully and participating in the discourses will lead the countries and continents to develop holistically. By doing so, we may transcend the traditional binary way of living life.

With these vignettes of background knowledge, I now move towards the translated works and made brief thematic analyses of Bijoy Satapathy's Odia plays *Kansara Atma* and *Kokua* here for the more significant sections and readership at the globe. In this book, I have translated *Kansara Atma* as *Soul of Kansa*, and the title of *Kokua* remains as it is when it is rendered from Odia into English. The *Soul of Kansa* is of two Acts. Act I highlights the Indian myth, as prescribed in the *Mahabharat*, of the conflict of vice and virtue. The protagonist, Kansa, stands for evil. This protagonist was of the *Dwapar Yuga* (Three thousand years earlier was in this Indian peninsula). A tyrannical ruler Kansa oppressed the ordinary people greatly. Kansa is not with us physically; his soul is very much alive in the society. The character Andhak represents the soul of Kansa.

Along with his associates like Bayasya, Chaturakshya and Councillors in the Royal Court, Andhak dominates and tortures the world. Anarchy, terror, menace, bloodshed, and corruption pervade everywhere in the society/world. Then Satyabrata and Dharmapal advocate for truth, peace, righteousness, and justice in the community that a good time is approaching soon. Then, a magical character joins the lap of a poor couple who are forcibly put in the prison, and his arrival makes all the prisoners accessible. The people get untied naturally from the tyrannical ruler, and his kingdom topples down. The Act II spells out the hazardous life of contemporary society. The characters Satyabrata and Dharmapal remain unaltered in the second part of the play. They are the true leaders of the community to stand against the industrialist-cum-politician Andhalochan and Chaturasen, a shareholder of his factory.

The Police Officer and the factory employee unquestionably support him, relegating to the background the sorrows and pains of the populace. A character, Biplab Ray, comes in contact with Satyabrata and Dharmapal, the prominent leaders of the Workers' Union, and motivates others in the factory. The supporters of Andhalochan plot a conspiracy against him, and Biplab Ray is dead before the worker's strike gets called off. The Police Officer is also in good liaison with the industrialist. The Police Officer files cases against Satyabrata and Dharmapal, considering them the murderers of Biplab Ray, and subsequently sends them to jail. They disagree at the points the industrialist, the factory owner has raised. The two characters always fight for the ordinary people, workers and labourers. They speak publicly; a time will come when the workers will rule over the country. With this Marxist ideology (trade union movement), they have been portrayed in the play. The workers should be aware of their natural rights and claim them through unions or organizations. This play juxtaposes both the incidents of the past and present world succinctly.

The playwright has used the transformation technique and the magic realism. In the first part, when the wife of Dhamapal gives birth, something uncanny is afoot. All the security guards die, and the prisoners are released. Moreover, Councillor-I is getting his eyes back because of the supernatural child. He told King Andhak once, "You are not on the path of truth and righteousness." The King ordered, then the people of the court to remove his eyes. The 'Royal Court' gets changed to the Factory of a Multi-National Company, the King Andhak becomes the industrialist-cum-Politician Andhalochan, and the Minister Chaturakshya becomes Chaturasen. One of the councillors of the court becomes the Police Officer and another an Employee of the Court, whereas Bayasya becomes the factory manager.

The second play, *Kokua*, revolves around Dhamaguda, a tribal village. Kokua is an imaginary, frightful, and mysterious character of the *Mahabharata*, one of the great epics of India. The *Mahabharata* of India has many regional versions in different languages. The *Kokua* anecdote is well described in Sarala Das's *Odia Mahabharata*. Kokua comes down, when the degree of doubt, disbelief, terror, murder, and anarchy overpowers the world. Because of the industrial growth and development, the tribes lose their land, rivers, brooks, forests, and simple lifestyles. Their mind gets polluted. The tribes are deprived of their natural rights. The issues of these locals are very beautifully reproduced. Shyamananda is the owner of the Ashram wherein Atanu was a disciple and later becomes the Police Inspector. At the same time, Ajay Marandi was also a disciple and later becomes a Naxal leader or Area Commander. Shyamananda's erstwhile belief was that he would guide rightly the students of this village to follow the path of non-violence. His dream is shattered in due course of time. Shibu (Also known as Sadashiba Rao) is a character supporting the Maoist movement.

Shibu and Ajay try their best to speak on behalf of the poor and the distressed tribes. When a factory is set up in their region, the people of Dhamaguda lose their lands. This play deals with the issue of displacement. The wretched people of the land have not received their compensation correctly. They suffer from the problem of rehabilitation. Their livelihood stops completely. At the cost of the forest, the factory is reinforced. The politician Gountia gets benefits from the industrial set-up. The refugee girl Monika comes in contact with Ajay, the Naxal leader, in Ashram, and love develops between the two. She gives birth to a child. At the end, Monika becomes a widow, and the question to the audience is whether the child will follow the path of violence or non-violence. This is what the mystery of the play is to the society. The firing of Police's pistols and the installation of landmines by the Naxalites disrupt the ordinary people's lifestyle. Every moment, they are terrified whether they will join the Naxals or come to the mainstream of society.

I have tried my best to keep the language as lucid as possible. While following the rules of equivalence and the rules of faithfulness between the Odia language and the English language, I came across some natural shifts. The culture-specific terms of the source language texts are retained as they are, while translating the text into English.

I deeply revere playwright Bijoy Kumar Satapathy for believing me to translate his texts carefully. He is a renowned professor of Odia Literature, retired from Utkal University. I convey my gratitude to Dr. Pradosh Kumar Swain, Assistant Professor, and Dr. Alok Baral, Assistant Professor, Department of Odia Language and Literature, Central University of Odisha, for helping me select this text for the stuff of my work.

I convey my heartfelt gratitude to Sri Satya Pattanaik, the director of Black Eagle Books, USA and Sri Ashok Parida of the publishing house for their kind consent to publish the texts in time.

Sanjeet Kumar Das

Soul of Kansa

Dramatis Personae

Andhak/Andhalochan

Chaturaksha/Chaturasen

Bayasya/Manager

Councillor-II/Factory Manager

Councillor-III/Police Officer

Rakshi/Constable

Dharmapala

Satyabrata

Stage Manager

Kansa

ACT - I
(Royal Court of the Emperor Andhak)

Scene-I

[A deep darkness pervades the stage. The music of a sad song mesmerizes the stage as if it were for many ages and centuries. A distressed cry of mournful souls is concealed in that music. After the stage light, the music immediately disappears. Stage manager stands in the middle of the stage. Coming to the front, he speaks for the audience.]

Stage Manager : Namaskar! The play we are going to stage before you is that the people experience the same feelings from the very inception of civilization. For this, there is bloodshed, revolution, the rise and fall of society, and so many. But what remain unaltered are exploitation, extortion, coercion, and authority's proclamation. From the beginning, the thirst for exploitation mingles with the human blood. It is primitive. The obstinate crown of the oppressor, his gold-decked throne, and unsealed swords glisten brightly and laugh at others' sorrows, sufferings and poverty. The flood of tears sheds. Here is also heard heavily the distressed heart's long breath. Nothing has changed. Everything is as usual. The chariot of time moves on and on. From the blocked agonies of human beings take birth the figures like Krushna, Rama, Narsingh, Nimain, Buddha, Chaitanya, and Christ. They have preached and proclaimed their sermons or messages earnestly. New hearts get streamed with the new lights, but something must still be fulfilled. The new ways of extortion and oppression and the obstinate crown of the new Emperor are self-expressing today. Kansa died, but from his soul, so many Kansas have been born for ages. Here is the cause of man's endless suffering. And the unfortunate Krushna! How helpless he is before the most powerful soul of Kansa! He can't do anything. He has descended on earth with many incarnations, but all these are fruitless. He gets defeated before Kansa.

[The Stage Manager disappears from the stage. Along with the flood of different coloured lights in cyclorama, there is fearsome laughter of Kansa. Then Kansa enters.]

Kansa : Hah...Hah...Hah (Laughter)

I am Kansa. I have no death! You want to establish virtue on this earth, destroying my material body in *Dwapar Yuga* and, as in the incarnation of Rama, killing Ravan in *Tretaya Yuga*. No…It's impossible. There is no end to our conflicts. My soul is invincible and immortal. You must come to this earth frequently in different forms. I will also live for ages in every atomic and subatomic particle of the planet and human blood vessels. I am more assertive and terrifying than the Creator. I don't care for Krishna, Parshuram and Buddha. I am stubborn and violent. I want to devour the whole world. All are my subjects, even God himself. Hah…Hah…Hah…

[The laughter of Kansa disappears from the stage. Then, there floats the stream of sad music on the stage for a while. After the light on stage, the Royal Court of Emperor Andhak is visible. Bayasya and other councillors are sitting there.]

Bayasya : (Standing) All the Councillors! Please be attentive to what I say. Nowhere have I seen a king like the Emperor Andhak, whenever I have travelled the earth and the sea. Thanks to his generosity and greatness, divinely blessed, he is the most powerful, even in the heaven and hell. No warrior parallels him, even in this Varun Kingdom.

Councilors II & III : (In unison) Absolutely!

Councillor II	:	He is like Duryodhan in pride, like Bali in grants and donations, like Brukodhar in power.
Councilor III	:	(Supporting his words) The Emperor Andhak is truly the live Vishnu, the live Supreme Soul (Over-soul). He is omniscient, omnipotent, and even more powerful than the Creator.
Bayasya	:	And Chturaksha!
Councilor II	:	He is the most violent and suitable associate of our King.
Bayasya	:	King Andhak and his Minister Chturaksha are present here. They are the priests of truth, righteousness and justice. Let's congratulate them in one voice.
Councilor II	:	(In unison) Let there be a victory for Emperor Andhak!
Councillor III	:	Let there be a victory for Great Minister Chaturaksha!
Councillor I	:	(He was listening to them patiently and suddenly got up.)
		O ...Shut up! Stop all this farce.
Bayasya	:	(wild and unruly tone) Satyabrata! We are the councillors. King's wealth and food nourish us. You are also the loyal and obedient servant to the Emperor, but...
Councillor I	:	I know that I am a councillor. I may be

	the loyal servant of the King. But is it my only identity? (very eagerly) Going against my conscience, I have followed the King's order for a long time, but today…
Bayasya	: (Browbeating) But today?
Councilor I	: It's unbearable. Injustice and oppression have crossed all the limits. I am forced to raise my voice against that.
Councilor II	: Satyabrata! You have forgotten that the most tyrannical King Andhak and his Minister can't forgive you.
Councilor III	: Who knows that you may be sentenced to death?
Councilor I	: I had long imprisoned myself to the boundary of falsehood. Today, that boundary has been disrupted. I am shining through the holy, glorious light of Truth and Justice. I am Satyabrata. Now, I realize the significance of the name today.
Bayasya	: (Laughing violently) Hah…hah…hah… it's enough. You are very talkative and nearing death soon.
Councillor I	: I don't care for death. It's a hundred times better to die than to live flattering or coaxing others. I want to live like a man.
Councilor III	: Perhaps you are mad, Satyabrata.
Councillor I	: I remind you again, 'learn how to live

		like a man. Stay away from blocking the paths of Truth and Justice by coaxing. One day, everything will be exposed in the light of truth.'
Bayasya	:	(Laughing)
Councillor II	:	(Laughing)
Councillor III	:	(Laughing)
		[All three are laughing in unison.]
Councillor I	:	I know very well that my voice of dissent is like a weak sparkle of light in the deep dense night. It may be extinguished. However, its message will give rise to hundreds of lamp lights. The darkness of night will vanish. Again, it will be a new morning with new light (exhilarated in happiness). Ah…how wonderful! There is no injustice. No,…flattering. There won't be many transgressions and adultery under the mask of morals and ethics. Rightly, that day, the man will learn how to live like a man.

[The arrival of the King on stage is hinted by the sounds of trumpet thrice. From the background, the multiple voices are heard: "Let there be a victory for the most powerful victor of all horizons or directions, the Emperor Andhak."]

Bayasya	:	Perhaps the Emperor Andhak has reached.

[The King enters the stage. He is steadfast now. His face seems to be dreadful. Minister Chaturaksha helps him show the road. He has a terrible physique and is a good swindler.]

Chaturaksha	:	(Leading the King toward the throne) Please be seated on the throne, the great Emperor! All the councillors eagerly wait for your arrival.
Andhak	:	(After sitting) The Great Minister Chaturaksha! All my dear councillors! Tell me how the Kingdom runs and how my subjects are.
Bayasya	:	Everything is fine. All is well, my Lord! Everywhere in the Kingdom, peace, justice, truth and righteousness pervade, like the *Rama Rajya* (State of fairness, good governance and lawfulness).
Councilor II	:	What Ram Rajya! Your Empire is far better and more prosperous than that.
Councillor III	:	You are a hundred times better warrior than Rama!
Councilor II	:	The God of Love, Kandarp, will be ashamed of looking at you for your handsome physique. You are so knowledgeable and virtuous. Rarely do we see a person like you in the world.
Andhak	:	(Smiling with pride) Hah…hah…hah…really, I am indeed the owner of enormous dignity, respect, wealth and prosperity.
Bayasya	:	Absolutely, My Lord! Your speech is as eternal as death.
Andhak	:	(getting up from the throne) Bayasya, you hear one more truth.

Bayasya	:	What's that, My Lord?
Andhak	:	I deny 'Death'. I have received this boon, having appeased all the Gods, through my meditation and prayer. I am *Mrutyunjayee* (Death can't touch me.) I am God and the God of kings. Hah…hah…hah…
Councilor II	:	(All three are in unison) Certainly!
Councilor III	:	(All three in unison) Certainly!
Bayasya	:	(All three in unison) Certainly!
Chaturaksha	:	(All three in unison) Certainly!
Councilor I	:	(In solemn tone) I strongly oppose this, My Lord!
Andhak	:	(Angrily) Who? (Moving two steps towards him) O…Satyabrata!
Chaturaksha	:	(Waving the sword) If the King orders; now I can behead you. You…Scoundrel!
Councillor I	:	The Great Minister! How come this language comes from your mouth? You are the well-wisher of the subjects, but…
Andhak	:	(Shouting) Shut up. Tell me why you become a traitor today.
Councillor I	:	My Lord! I am not a traitor. Your governance has displeased me. In the Kingdom, corruption and anarchy are perceived everywhere. The truth, righteousness, sympathy and forgiveness are seldom seen. A blind administration runs in the Kingdom. Coaxing and flat-

	tering of the King are the duties of the councillors and his governance is directed towards the hell now-a-days.
Andhak & others in one voice	: Satyabrata!
Councillor I	: I am very conscious. Perhaps I will be punished severely for my words. But remember My Lord and my dear councillors, that time will come one day. I can hear that vibration. He is coming with a new morning song…. Rightly, that day…
Chaturaksha	: My Lord, before I listen to anything more…(He touches the unsealed sword to the throat of Satyabrata.)
Bayasya	: Unbearable, unbearable this speech, My Lord! (In unison)
Councilor-II	: Unbearable, unbearable this speech, My Lord! (In unison)
Councillor III	: Unbearable, unbearable this speech, My Lord! (In unison)
Bayasya	: Let him be punished soon.
Andhak	: (with a tone of excitement) Minister Chaturaksha!
Chaturaksha	: My Lord!
Andhak	: At the Royal Courtyard in broad daylight, remove his eyes. Let him roam with his bloodstained eyes from door to door. This is what the extreme punishment I

	order you now. Minister Chaturaksha, You execute the order soon, please.
Councillor	: My Lord! I am not a traitor. I have told you the hard, bitter truth. Think of it again, my Lord.
Andhak	: Hah...Hah...Hah...
	Andhak never withdraws or takes back his punishment. He is more terrible than *Yamraj* (God of Death), and his punishment is extremely severe. Hah...hah...hah...
Chaturaksha	: (Rudely) Security! (A sentinel enters.) Take this traitor and remove his eyes. Then, throw him on the road towards the Royal Palace. Let him loiter here and there as a blind person. Let Satyabrata explore the truth with his blind eyes.

[*Satyabrata ventilates his anger for the King loudly, while the sentinel takes him away.*]

Bayasya	: The right decision of His Majesty, the Emperor.
Councillor II	: The right decision of His Majesty, the Emperor.
Councillor III	: The right decision of His Majesty, the Emperor.
Andhak	: Hah...Hah...Hah...
	(Taking a turn to the discourse) Yes, Minister Chaturaksha!
	Last night I had a strange nightmare.

Chaturaksha	:	(Being surprised) A strange nightmare!
Andhak	:	Yes, the great Minister! On the outskirts of this capital, a poor couple will give birth to a child. He will be the assassin of my life. He will be the Yamaraj to me.

[All in unison, start laughing sarcastically.]

Chaturaksha	:	The assassin of the mightiest warrior of the warriors, the great Emperor Andhak! Hah...hah...It makes me laugh. Again, he will be born into a poverty-stricken family. Hah...hah...hah...
Bayasya	:	My Lord! If you have any doubt regarding this, let all the poor people of the Kingdom be imprisoned...
Councillor II	:	Let them be thrown into prison.
Councilor III	:	If the prison is not enough for that, let them be killed brutally.
Andhak	:	Good proposal. (In commanding voice) Minister Chaturaksha! Start your expedition with the army at this moment. Let the Kingdom be spread with the devastation of the strongest Emperor, Andhak. Let them all realize how powerful I am. Let them feel how terrible Andhak is, like death. Hah...hah...hah. Nobody will come to this earth as an enemy to him.

[The stage light is off while Andhak, Chaturaksha, Bayasya and Councilors laugh in unison.]

[END]

SCENE-II

[Here's again the same Royal court. Minister Chaturaksha sits. Dharmapal stands in front of him. He is the poorest person in the Kingdom. His hands and legs are manacled.]

Chaturaksha	:	(Roaring) Stubborn Dharmapal!
Dharmapal	:	I am not stubborn. I am a poor subject of the Kingdom, and by nature, I am very humble.
Chaturaksha	:	(Sarcastically) A poor, humble subject! Are you sure that you don't advise the people to be revolutionary in their approach? Don't you motivate them to stand and raise their voice against the King?
Dharmapal	:	False, Sir. I haven't taught them anything except the advice of righteousness.
Chaturaksha	:	Are you sure you have not seen a dream wherein a child is born in your family with brilliance and prosperity, and he will be the assassin of the Emperor later?
Dharmapal	:	(In submissive tone) This is false, Sir. I

am sonless, worthless, and a poor fellow. That night, in an auspicious moment, I had a dream. (Crying) I am blessed with a son who is very righteous and with all the good qualities of humanity. After he is born, the whole surroundings are lit immediately.

Chaturaksha : Similarly, Emperor Andhak had seen the same dream too. The son of a poor, distressed subject will be the cause of his death. That's why, only that's why we are imprisoning you now. Here is a strange similarity between you and the Emperor regarding that dream.

Dharmapal : My Lord! I am an inferior and innocent subject. My wife is pregnant. Let us be released at this critical moment instead of imprisoning here, Sir.

Chaturaksha : It's impossible, Dharmapal. Once your son takes birth, we will kill him, cruelly strangling his throat. How come he will be engaged in regicide?

Dharmapal : (surrendering in a submissive tone) No…no…no…I am sonless, and please forgive me. God can't tolerate this injustice, Sir.

Chaturaksha : God…Hah…Hah…indecision…There is only one God, Dharmapal! He is the Emperor Andhak.

[The Emperor Andhak and Bayasya enter.]

Andhak	:	Who's this, Chaturaksha?
Chaturaksha	:	He is Dharmapal, the most distressed poor subject of the Kingdom. In line with your dream, he will be blessed with a son who will be your assassin later. Along with him, his wife, who is pregnant, is also imprisoned. I have explained them our command too. Once his son is born in the darkness of prison, we will kill him by strangling him.
Andhak	:	(Laughing loudly) Do you have anything to say?
Dharmapal	:	(Crying) My Lord! If there is truth, righteousness, and justice in the world, then…

[Without giving him any scope, Andhak roars violently.]

Andhak	:	Shut up. You are talking of truth, righteousness, and justice. I am the symbolic head of all those qualities. I represent all of these attributes. Listen to me, Dharmapal! Andhak never tolerates his opponent. Besides, your son will be the assassin of the Emperor. Hah…hah…hah…You will suffer in the lonely dreary of the prison. If you and your wife get released from that by any chance and your wife will give birth to a child, but we will kill your son cruelly.
Dharmapal	:	(Mournfully) His Majesty!
Andhak	:	(To Chaturaksha) Take Dharmapal

with you, Chaturaksha. Torture him along with his wife insolently. Yes, you administer the subjects who raise their voice against the Emperor's decision firmly with cruelty.

[Chaturaksha leaves the spot with Dharmapal.]

Bayasya : (Laughing) The Emperor is relatively safe!.

[Councillor II and Councillor III enter.]

Councillor II : Destruction, My Lord!

Andhak : (with anger loudly) Destruction!

Councillor III : Councillor Satyabrata is blind and now suffers from royal punishment. He announces the revolutionary message from door to door with his begging bowl.

Andhak : Imprison Sataybrata. Control the subjects vehemently with my army. It's my order. Today, Andhak is violent Victor *Yamraj*.

[Councillor II and Councillor III leave the place out of fear.]

Bayasya : The blind Satyabrata will publicize the revolutionary speech.

Andhak : We can't take this information lightly, Bayasya. The subjects are ready to revolt. So what?

Bayasya : His Majesty! We will kill them like the insects. Yes, My Lord, I have an idea…

Andhak : Express it confidently.

Bayasya	:	You have forgotten your recreation and lavish lifestyle for the last few days. Today, can I make some arrangements for you?
Andhak	:	Yes, Bayasya. I was deeply thoughtful for the last few days. My dance bar has also been silent. I have enjoyed many nubile ladies and many beautiful girls, but...
Bayasya	:	What's then, My Lord?
Andhak	:	I have heard that you are blessed with a pretty daughter...
Bayasya	:	(Being terrified) My Lord!
Andhak	:	Yes, Bayasya! I want your beautiful daughter for this night only.
Bayasya	:	(Closing his ears and in a mournful voice) Before that, please, you kill me, My Lord! Yes, please kill me.
Andhak	:	You see, Bayasya! You are nourished in the royal food. My order must be executed. (He leaves.)
Bayasya	:	Yes, My Lord! I must obey your command. I am an employee of the court. I don't have freedom. I am not independent. I am weak. I can't revolt. Yes, Andhak, to your Hall of Entertainment, I will send my daughter. I am Bayasya. Who else is here, other than me, to make you happy?

[He laughs and subsequently cries.]

Light off

SCENE-III

[The same atmosphere here pervades. Some seats are withdrawn from the Royal Court after the stage is flooded with lights. On the whole, some changes are perceived. The Emperor Andhak and Minister Chaturaksha enter at that time.]

Andhak : Minister Chaturaksha!

Chaturaksha : His Majesty!

Andhak : Today's meeting seems to be very lonely. There is deadly silence in the surroundings and a strange transformation in the Kingdom. A cold war is likely to happen against me. What's the cause, Chaturaksha?

Chaturaksha : I have also marked that a shade of terror and apprehension overpowers the Kingdom with its wings spread.

Andhak : (Experiencing terror and apprehension within) terror and suspense! (Avoiding all this later) No, no…I…I…am all right. I am fine. (Shouting) Chaturaksha! You are only the eye, nose and ear of the Emperor, Andhak. Dominate this

		transformation strongly at your level. Let the Kingdom be converted into a cremation ground of brown and red colour dust.
Chaturaksha	:	My Lord, I have executed all this. The whole Kingdom is now a prison. The atmosphere is echoed with the unbearable cries of distress of the subjects day and night. Still…
Andhak	:	Still?
Chturaksha	:	Still, it seems to me, if the subjects accept all the tortures, the discontentment of their souls has already given birth to their silent protest. They have disobeyed all the orders of the Emperor. Who knows, your dream may be…
Andhak	:	(Being agitated and terrified) Can the dream I saw be true, Chaturaksha? (Being conscious of his state) No…No…I am the most powerful tyrant ruler of King Andhak. I am mrityunjayee (the conqueror of death). I have a strong army. Again, I have the assassin. Hah… hah…hah…Listen to me, Chaturaksha!
Chaturaksha	:	My Lord!
Andhak	:	At this moment, come with me. I will kill Dharmapal and his wife, strangling in my own hands. (He becomes firm and determined.)This can also be a good plan for preventing their child from entering this world. But I am so weak.

Is the Emperor Andhak afraid of death? No, Let Dharmapal be given a chance to prove himself in sorrows and sufferings of the prison; how is his son going to be the assassin of the Emperor? I will kill that newborn child brutally. After that Dharmapal...subsequently his wife...

[He laughs violently.]

Chaturaksha : *Maharaj*, the future child, has already taken birth from the sorrows and sufferings. Otherwise, it couldn't have happened.

Andhak : (Indistinctive cry of distress) Oh... That future child who will be the assassin of the King. Though I try hard, I am unable to forget this excitement and apprehension of my death. That child...I don't know what to do next. In the babbling sounds of the newborn child, my crown, gold-decked throne, unsealed sword... (He gets agitated gradually.), Well! Minister Chaturaksha! What's about the councillor Satyabrata?

Chaturaksha : Maharaj! After being blind, on the outskirts of the capital, he lives begging for alms. Sometimes, he speaks indistinctively like a lunatic- the illuminated light of truth will certainly come down on earth one day.

Andhak : Oh...

(He controls him firmly like the thunderbolt.) I am...yes...yes...I am...Truth, Justice, and Righteousness...Hah...hah...hah

Chaturaksha	:	Certainly, Maharaj!
		[At this time, the sentinel enters.]
Sentinel	:	(Congratulating him) Let there be a victory for the Emperor!
Andhak	:	What's new information?
Sentinel	:	Maharaj! The wife of Dharmapal gives birth to a son in the prison. The cry of the newborn makes the prison noisy and lit, too. The shackles of Dharmapal and all other prisoners are untied. They are free now. The closed doors of the prison are open now astonishingly.
Andhak	:	(Roaring) Sentinel!
Chaturaksha	:	(Roaring) Sentinel!
Sentinel	:	(Being terrified) Maharaj! The child's cry was fearsome. The army prepared with armour. But...
Andhak	:	(Helplessly) But...
Sentinel	:	They have all been found dead. Impossible! That child is divinely blessed. The glowing light streaming from his body takes their lives.
Chaturaksha	:	Then, will that dream be true, Maharaj?
Andhak	:	Now I am completely helpless, Chatruraksha. The only way for me is to escape.

[The scream of the child is echoed. Andhak, Chaturaksha and the Sentinel are disturbed.]

Chaturaksha	:	You can hear, Maharaj! The cry of this child is the assassin of the Emperor in future. But, in his voice, there is a powerful attraction, as if we were being handicapped and hypnotised. Someone withdraws energy from us.
		[Councilor II and Councilor III reach the stage hurriedly.]
Councilor II	:	Maharaj! The Minister Chaturaksha quits the place quickly. The whole army gets neutralized after the child takes birth in this world.
Councillor III	:	The shackles of the hundreds of prisoners are automatically removed and untied. This news has been spread first like lightning throughout the Kingdom.
Councilor II	:	The people are excited and revolutionary in their approach. They are united and violently surging towards the capital.

[From the background, the cry of a child is heard along with the voice of excitement of the people. The Councilor I, Satyabrata, enters.]

Satyabrata	:	The Emperor Andhak, Minister Chturaksha and my dear Councilors! That day I told you that I would return to you when everything was exposed in the streaming light of truth.
Andhak	:	(Being surprised) Satyabrata! You…

Councillor I	:	One day, you have punished me. My fault was that I was on the path of righteousness and nearing Truth and Justice. I wouldn't say I liked coaxing or flattery.
Andhak	:	You were blind. How did you get back your eyes? Surprising!
Councilor I	:	The eyes of Truth, Justice and Righteousness can't be destroyed. After the birth of this supernatural child, I have been blessed with my eyes to see the world again. My understanding is more substantial, sharper and brighter than earlier. Before my eyes, there is a signal of a new age, a brilliant crimson-coloured sun. He has already taken birth as a leader of revolution and salvation.

[The child's cry is accompanied by the slogan of the united voice. Dharmapal enters.]

Chaturaksha	:	(Shouting) Who…Dharmapal?
Dharmapal	:	Yes, Sir, I am Dharmapal. A distressed poor fellow has been thrown into prison without any fault or crime. Please visit both Emperor Andhak and Minister Chaturaksha to see how my dream comes true. (With eagerness) At the lap of my wife is that supernatural child. He will be the end to this monarchy of darkness. The old tradition is being destroyed.
Andhak	:	(Being overwhelmed in sadness) I

	know, Dharmapal. Your dream and Satyabrata's forecasting are true now. Chaturaksha! I am helpless today. My happiness and prosperity and my relatives gradually disappear from my sight. Now I am alone.
Chaturaksha	: I have been vanquished. All my efforts to control agitation are in vain. You must have heard, Maharaj! Our dear Bayasya committed suicide out of sorrow, insult and anger.
Andhak	: I am well aware of the cause of his death. He has chosen that path to disobey the stern, cruel command of the Emperor. (Twisting the mood of the discourse) I am a sinner. My tendency mainly drives me. Oh...

[A group of people enter the stage. In their hands are swords, sticks, shields, spears, and knives. Some indicators are with torch lights of victory. Now the stage lights are off. The faces of the characters present on the stage are visible only in the torch lights.]

Andhak	: Andhak! Your blind governance comes to an end. Minister Chaturaksha's art of cheating the ordinary people was in the last stage today. (Pointing fingers towards the agitated mass) Manacle both of them. Please search for the followers and the attendants in the palace and the Hall of Entertainment and imprison them all. The people will decide and pass judgment for them. A new system will come to the country. The people will govern themselves.

[All the characters on stage encircle Andhak and Chaturaksha. Their hands are manacled. The light focuses on King Andhak's face. Others stand idly.]

Andhak : Hah...Hah...Hah!

People will decide about me. Will Andhak accept defeat? No, it's impossible. This is a temporary defeat and a transformation. Perhaps he will die in today's revolution, but he will take birth on this earth in a new form. He will continue anarchy and exploitation ceaselessly without any opposition. Hah...hah...hah..

[The stage light is off, along with Andhak's laughter. After the stage light, Kansa stands in the middle of the stage.]

Kansa : I am Kansa. I live in every atomic and sub-atomic particle of the world. My soul is hidden or dormant in the unknown niches of the human mind. My fight with Krishna never ends or will end. Sometimes, Kansa will win, or sometimes Krishna will win. My journey is irresistible. I am a terror and invincible. I am also with an indomitable spirit. Hah...hah...Hah!

Light off

ACT-II

(The office room of Andhalochan Sahasamalla near his factory)

Scene-I

[Deep darkness prevails over the stage. A musical note of sadness mesmerizes the whole atmosphere. After the stage light, it is observed that the Stage Manager stands in the middle of the stage. Two steps moving forward the audience, he starts.]

Stage Manager : Ladies and Gentlemen! We have staged before you a play comprising a King, a Minister, and a buffoon of the past. Don't think that the play ends here. Will you leave the place only having a glance over the history? Then, it will be considered that we have staged a play with a king, a minister, and his councillors. That's not over. We could have produced and directed what our ancestors had experienced. Now, I will take you to a new set-up. We may not see Andhak, Chaturaksha, Bayasya, or Councilors of the Royal Court there, but we will meet the characters of their same race or nature. Then the same story is also retold differently! One group will be 'the oppressed'; the other will be 'the oppressor'. The flogging on the heart and tearful eyes gives birth to a revolution. Sometimes, the revolution may be suppressed forcibly; otherwise, the ruler must surrender before the revolution. There is no difference, but it is the same story. The exploitation or extortion changes its form based on the situation. Now, I march ahead. This time, in the play, instead of King Andhak and his councillors, you will see Andhalochan and his followers. Are they the only priests of democracy? Won't we gauze their characters?

[After the Stage Manager leaves the spot, the light is off. In that darkness, different musical instruments are played. On the stage, light focuses on the Office attached to the factory of Andhalochan Sahasmalla. He is sitting in the Office. He is a renowned industrialist and a politician, too.

Along with him, Chaturasen Senapati is also sitting there. Chaturasen is a shareholder of the factory, a companion to Andhalochan in the field of politics, and a police officer is also there. They are engrossed in an important matter. Intermittently, they are taking cigarettes and creating spiral columns of smoky air playfully in the surroundings. An employee of the factory stands submissively beside them.]

Andhalochan	:	The election is recently over. Now I am sure that we will face an intense fight.
Chaturasen	:	If needed, we will spend money lavishly. We have to win it by any means.
Police Officer	:	If you win this time, you will get a post in the higher cadre of the Ministry.
Employee	:	The country needs the most talented persons like you.
Andhalochan	:	By the way I have no greed for power. My first duty and mission is to serve the country.
Chaturasen	:	By nature, sir is entirely different. I have friendship with him for the last twenty years. (To the Police Officer and the Employee) You, the two, are unaware of his personality. He is combined in one of the qualities of a learned man, a leader, and an orator. He is also a freedom fighter.
Police Officer	:	Yes, Sir. I am well aware of this. Before I joined here, while posted at a different place, I had been acquainted with his high recognition and praise throughout the country. His photos and the central ideas of his speeches were published in the newspapers.
Employee	:	Be sure, Sir. You have come to this police station recently. You have heard about him, now you will realize what kind of personality he is. He is both the father

and the mother of his factory workers.

Andhalochan : What have I received after sacrificing a lot for the people? They are talking of my blemishes everywhere. It has been a common rule of the country. Now, nobody pays respect to justice and ideals.

Employee : A handful of people in the factory have spoiled the entire ambience, Sir. Only revolution, strike, agitation…

Andhalochan : (Firmly) Perhaps they don't know. After suspending them, I can appoint new persons in their place now.

Chaturasen : If this indiscipline continues in the factory for some days, this will be the best strategy.

Police Officer : Well, what are their basic problems?

Chaturasen : Sir, their problems are to increase their salary, to give them a bonus, and to sanction a more significant number of holidays. Yes, Sir. We will release the salary, based upon the factory's turnover. Forming a "Workers' Union", they have raised their voice against us.

Police Officer : Well, have they formed the Union?

Chaturasen : In this democratic country, if people want, they can form a Union or a *Sangha*. After that, you will see strikes, agitation, campaign, and procession. The country mostly runs with these issues.

Andhalochan	:	Listen to me, Chaturasen. You do one thing. Let a communiqué be released on behalf of the administration that we can't give anything more from our side by any means. If they want to stay, they can, otherwise let them quit the factory and join at any other place. I have invested lakhs of rupees for this factory. Again, I will never surrender before the workers.
Employee	:	Sir, how many people are so generous like you in this country? I have tried my best to make them understand. But none of them hears me. One young man has come from somewhere and incited all the workers in the factory. Inspired by him, Satyabrata and Dharmapal are leading here to motivate others.
Andhalochan	:	Well, who's that guy to advise the workers for revolution?
Employee	:	Well, Biplab Ray.
Andhalochan	:	Biplab Ray?
Chaturasen	:	He has very bizarre movements. He is well educated.
Andhalochan	:	But what will he earn, if the workers are united?
Chaturasen	:	His arguments are very strange.
Employee	:	Sir, that day, he said the whole factory would be under the workers' control.
Andhalochan	:	Hah...Hah...Hah...Yes, the factory was

built in the workers' capital. So it should be under their control.

Police Officer : Sir, don't worry about this. I will take care of it. Well, if you want, now I can arrest that stubborn guy.

Andhalochan : No, no, not at all. We should not be so reactive right now. Moreover, we have to wait for the declaration of election's result. This may create a bad impression in the people's mind. If the situation worsens, I will seek your help immediately.

Police Officer : Sir, I am grateful to you forever. I will always remember your help. Had you not interfered in the last incident, I would have been completely ruined and gone to hell.

Andhalochan : Please listen to me. The people who always stick to justice are stupid. Your people have searched and red-handed a hotel that day. They have also seized something. Have you ever thought of the disastrous consequence of that action? The whole city was in commotion.

Police Officer : Since that day, I have been your disciple, and you are my teacher. I don't have 'any say' if anything happens in that hotel.

Chaturasen : Apart from that, we have already accepted that we will share with you the profit that the hotel will have.

Police Officer	:	Sir, that's not important. I am always at your service.
Andhalochan	:	(To Employee) Yes, you do what I say. You, on behalf of our administration, influence the workers. If needed, we will spend a lot. If any conspiracy is plotted against the factory, bring the same to our notice soon.
Employee	:	Yes, Sir! (While leaving, parting his hair) yes, what I say here is…
Andhalochan	:	What?
Employee	:	I have a request.
Chaturasen	:	You need some money.
Andhalochan	:	How much?
Employee	:	Sir!
Andhalochan	:	You take the amount you want from the Manager. You will concentrate upon our work.

[That Employee leaves. Andhalochan says to the Police Officer.]

Well, you may leave now. I will call you in case of any urgency. Or if you have any problem, contact me anytime. I have to put pressure on the top floor. Don't worry, go on working firmly. I stand by you. Tomorrow I have to attend the election meeting. Your people, deployed at the meeting venue should take care of the situation. There should not be any disturbance.

Police Officer	:	Well, no need to be worried, Sir. I have a request. If you don't mind-
Chaturasen	:	Is it related to finance matters?

Police Officer	:	Yes, of course.
Andhalochan	:	How much?
Police Officer	:	Now I have already booked my vehicle.
Andhalochan	:	Oh, I see! (He laughs loudly later.)

Please hear, take the amount that you need from us. Yes, there is no need to return the same. I have considered you my bosom friend.

[He laughs. Chaturasen and the Police Officer also join him.]

Light off

SCENE-II

[Andhalochan and Chaturasen talk to each other on the stage light.]

Chaturasen : Sir, your apprehension has become true now.

Andhalochan : I know. Try to think of the strategy to trap them all. Otherwise, our name, fame and institute will ruin and vanish. Apart from that, we have the elections ahead. What will the people think about me? Anyhow, we have to suppress this. I am unable to give you time for this. I am busy with the Party's work. You take the whole responsibility of dismantling the workers' strike.

Chaturasen : Sir, the strike has already been for ten days. The workers and the labourers have become undisciplined and rude in their approach. We have had a significant loss for the last few days. I am planning what to do next at this juncture of time.

Andhalochan : Chaturasen, you have already been with me for the last twenty years as

	a companion of my political life. You are my bosom friend and, again, a shareholder of my factory. How can I say what you have to do at this moment? Your name is Chaturasen. You justify your name. First of all, adopt the formula of 'Labour Aristocracy'. If it doesn't work, smash them all. You will spend the amount of money needed for this.
Chaturasen	: That stubborn guy Biplab Ray is the cause of all this. His brilliant speech on the public platform ignited a spark of light for revolution among workers in the factory. He says, "One day for the entire country there will be the Government of workers and labourers, and he starts his experiment first in this factory."
Andhalochan	: Hah…Hah…it may be his incoherent talk. Yes, for this you can call the Manager. After consulting him, you do what stringent actions you want to take against them. I will leave for Delhi tonight. There is an emergency meeting of our Party. One more point…
Chatursen	: What's that, please?
Andhalochan	: (In low tone) What's about our 'Gold Export'?
Chaturasen	: Yes, we have already arranged the 'Gold Biscuits', and in turn, we will receive

		the foreign exchange of approximately Thirty Lakh Dollars. With that, our people have left for Bombay today. The Police Officer has already taken care of the Underground of our hotel and is vigilant about this. We are safe now. Then it's heard…
Andhalochan	:	Hah…Hah…Hah (Laughing)
		The people of the Opposition Party will engage the C.B.I. for this. An Enquiry Committee may be constituted. Listen to me, Chaturasen! Andhalochan Sahasmalla is not so stupid that he will amass a lot. All the higher officials are within my ambit. I may be defeated in the election. I will stop them with my financial deals. I throw parties for the Governmental Officials and donate a lot to charitable organizations.

[The Manager of the factory enters. He is an age-old man. He says Pranam to both of them.]

Andhalochan	:	What steps have you undertaken to end the strike that has been continued for the last ten days, Manager Babu?
Manager	:	Yes, Sir. I tried my best to explain them all, but all my efforts went in vain, Sir.
Andhalochan	:	(In solemn voice) Manager.
Manager	:	(Being afraid of) Yes, Sir!
Andhalochan	:	Do you know how much our factory has lost for the last ten days?

Manager	:	Approximately above 1.5 Crores
Andhalochan	:	I will recover all this from your salary.
Manager	:	(with mournful tone) Yes, I will die!
Andhalochan	:	(Roaring) Bastard! Ungrateful, treacherous fellow! I will expel you from the job at this moment. You were loitering like a pauper on the road that day. I appointed you here. Giving you promotions in the factory, I have made you the factory manager. Is this the consequence of that? Isn't it a loss of lakhs of rupees to appoint you in my factory? (Being annoyed) All nonsense!
Chaturasen	:	Had you been a little conscious, the possibility of strike could have been avoided.
Manager	:	Yes, the stubborn guy Biplab Ray leads the strike. Dharmapal and Satyabrata, two leaders of the Workers' Union, assist him for this.
Andhalochan	:	Oh, I see!
		Yes, Chaturasen! (He whispers something in his ears.) Our first target is Biplab and then others. Yes, you bring false allegations against Dharmapal and Satyabrata. Assembling a group of people against them will prove that they are wrong. I will suspend them. I will also lodge a case against them in the Police station. Go, go immediately.

		Consult Chaturasen and do what you want to.
Manager	:	(While leaving, he stops for a while.) Sir!
Chturasen	:	Do you say me something?
Manager	:	Yes, everything is ready in the Factory Bungalow.
Chatursen	:	(Having understood) Oh…yes…yes.
		Well, you leave now. (The Manager leaves. He talks to Andhalochan.) Sir, today at 7.30 P.M., Meenakshi Bahidar will be waiting for you.
Andhalochan	:	Ok, Yes…But…
Chaturasen	:	Tomorrow morning, she will receive the cheque of Six Lakhs.
Andhalochan	:	Her poor father is without money for the marriage.
Chaturasen	:	Then, it's well. At the cost of Six Lakhs, you will gratify your lust with her for the whole night. That amount will be enough for her marriage. Nobody will know this.
Andhalochan	:	(Laughing violently) Hah…Hah…You are truly clever, Chaturasen.
		[While laughing, the light is off.]

SCENE-III

[Chaturasen and the Manager are sitting at the factory's Office.]

Chaturasen : Sir leaves for Delhi this morning.

Manager : Here, at the Workers' Union Office, the fire of discontentment escalates. It gets peaked day by day. There is no question of compromise.

Chaturasen : We have to execute our earlier plan. Otherwise, there's no other way for us.

Manager : Sir, that guy Biplab Ray is delivering a brilliant speech publicly. He is a good orator. He has hypnotized all.

Chaturasen : There is no need for any further discussion here.

[The Manager is aware of situation. Dharmapal and Satyabrata enter.]

Satyabrata : (To the Manager) Sir, have you called both of us?

Chaturasen : Please be seated. (To both Dharmapala and Satyabrata)

Manager : We have called you here to discuss the issues about the strike.

Chaturasen	:	You see, Satyabrata! You are an honest worker. We have enough sympathy for you. I have been forced to change my attitude towards you, since the day you have started revolting against the factory.
Satyabrata	:	You believe you will stay peacefully, knowing about the strike, Sir. But, remember, I haven't done any harm to anyone. When I was innocent, I was completely unaware of your secret plans. But, now I can understand your true nature.
Chaturasen	:	Stop it.
Manager	:	(Changing his mood) Be calm and silent, Satyabrata! We will find out an amicable solution or make a compromise for the workers' strike. Today, Andhalochan has gone to Delhi for an emergency meeting, and we have been handed over the factory's responsibility for a decision to the strike raised so far.
Dharmapal	:	Our Workers' Union has always sought this from the very beginning. But you are all withdrawing from this.
Satyabrata	:	The workers are on hunger strike. Forget about their demands. Have you ever visited the spot where they usually sit to attend to their issues sympathetically?
Dharmapal	:	How far is it justified for him to escape

		from this place without addressing their issues? What do you want?
Manager	:	You don't understand, Dharmapal. You are floating like a boat in the stream. We have sympathy for both of you. You are both talented.
Dharmapal	:	Leave coaxing. Anyway, please tell us why you have called us here.
Manager	:	We want you to call off the strike.
Satyabrata	:	Before that, you must accept all the demands of the Workers' Union.
Chaturasen	:	You see, Satyabrata and Dharmapal! We like both of you. Andhalochan Babu also likes you both. For that, before he leaves for Delhi, he has approved your promotion. I request both of you to stop the strike.
Manager	:	Yes, we have made other arrangements for you, too. You stay away from the strike and help others withdraw from it.
Dharmapal	:	(Angrily) You are depriving us of our natural rights with this temptation. We hate money and position. We don't want to live through flattery. We will live like human beings.
Chaturasen	:	Dharmapal!
Satyabrata	:	Yes, we will revolt until our demands get fulfilled. We won't care for any danger.
Manager	:	You need to remember Satyabrata.

		Andhalochan Sahasmalla won't forgive you. You have to face the music for this.
Dharmapal	:	You can't suppress us by browbeating. All the workers are united. One day, all the workers of the country will be united and claim their genuine rights.
Manager	:	This is the speech of your Guru, Biplab Ray.
Satyabrata	:	Biplab Ray is not a man but truly a godlike figure. He denies coaxing and flattery. He is overwhelmed by the formation of a new society. He has not learnt to live licking the feet of the bourgeois class, the exploiters. He has motivated us. He has made us aware of our power.
Chatursen	:	Satyabrata! Leave the place immediately. I will take serious action against you.
Dharmapal	:	Don't lose your temper, Sir. For the downfall of Bureaucracy, not only Biplab Ray alone but so many soldiers like us are behind. Your decline starts soon.

[After they leave, the stage light is off.]

SCENE-IV

[Andhalochan, Chaturasen and the Manager are talking to each other at the Office of their Factory.]

Andhalochan : How far have you been successful?

Manager : Everything is all right. At any moment, the agitated workers may enter our Office. On behalf of the Workers' Union, a condolence meeting is organized.

Andhalochan : Don't worry. If they cross the limit, we will assure them of an independent inquiry.

Chaturasen : (Laughing loudly) That is the best way of democracy. Till the report comes out, all of them will forget the matter.

Andhalochan : By the way, I have won the election. With the influence of higher officials, the case can be dismissed.

Chaturasen : Biplab Ray is murdered so cautiously that it will be tough for the workers to identify the culprit. You know what I have done (Whispering to him). I have also planned accordingly to send Satyabrata and Dharmapal to be handcuffed and dragged to the jail.

Manager	:	After murdering Biplab, our people have kept different objects at Satyabrata's house and Dharmapal's house too. That will be enough for the officers to declare them the main culprits of this murder.
Andhalochan	:	Well, I appreciate your intelligence.
Chaturasen	:	On behalf of our Office, I think you have informed the police before they do so. Then, the Police Officer is with us. He also receives the percentage from our smuggling.
Andhalochan	:	Bravo! You are my actual shareholder. Because of you, I have won the elections. Again, for you, I will be able to call off the workers' strike.
		[Outside the Office, there is the voice of agitation.]
Manager	:	Sir, perhaps they have reached us.
Andhalochan	:	Let them come. Who cares?
		[Dharmapal and Satyabrata rush to the Office.]
Andhalochan	:	(Having seen him) Come, Satyabrata. You come, Dharmapal. What's your problem?

[Outside the Office, the slogan of the agitated workers continues.]

Satyabrata	:	(Speaking firmly and angrily) You have to reply to this today.
Dharmapal	:	Yes, correct answer. Otherwise, all the workers will ruin your factory and this

		duplex (of the office). Your followers have murdered Biplab Ray brutally. To take revenge for that, we are here…
Andhalochan	:	(Roaring) You shut up. You know whom you are saying. Perhaps you don't remember Andhalochan Sahasamalla. Do you know what kind of punishment is for the stubborn guy like you?
Manager	:	The factory will take serious action against you immediately.
Chaturasen	:	You will be suspended from the service soon.
Satyabrata	:	You are the scoundrel to be flattered and the person who doesn't understand anything except power. Till our hands are active and functional, we will never be hungry for power.
Dharmapal	:	What had he done to you? He had united the poor and distressed workers and advised them for their natural rights. He had shown them the way to live. He has served the poor and the wretched, staying at the slum. Engaging the people, you have murdered him.
Manager	:	Listen to me, Dharmapal! Before the court, both of you are the culprits. You can't deny this. You are both responsible for the murder of Biplab Ray. We have enough proof for this.
Chturasen	:	I can say confidently; there was also the

conflict among the workers regarding leadership.

Andhalochan : You can remember, both of you were called for an amicable solution to the workers' agitation. On some proposals, you have agreed to us in the two-party discussion. Of course, your self-interest was involved in it. Biplab Ray may not agree to the same. For that…

Satyabrata : You are mistaken. We didn't accept your proposals at all and returned. You had also offered us so many temptations. But we rejected them all.

Manager : Have the patience to listen to me, Dharmapal.

[He shows a paper.]

You see, you had signed here in some of the proposals. You had also agreed to call off the strike without fulfilling the demands.

Dharmapal : This doesn't seem right. This conspiracy is plotted against us.

[The Police Officer and a constable enter at this time.]

Andhalochan : Please come here, please come.

Police Officer : We have received a report, "There was a murder last night at your factory." Having investigated the slum of the workers, we have seized the bloodstained knives and some other objects of suspicion from two of your

	workers. We have heard that those who murdered him were the leaders of the Workers' Union and the one who was murdered, too.
Manager	: Yes, Sir, this was the competition for leadership. These are the two fellows before you. They also threaten us after committing the crime.
Police Officer	: Well! These are more dangerous people. (To Satyabrata and Dharmapal) You want to say something in this regard.
Satyabrata	: We are not the culprits, Sir.
Police Officer	: But we have enough proof against you.
Dharmapal	: These are all false allegations. They have murdered Biplab Ray, but we are blamed for that. He was our bosom friend and colleague. We can't do this.
Police Officer	: Some of the witnesses or workers of the factory have reported against you. They had seen you roaming here and there in the slum that night when there was the murder.
Satyabrata	: (The flood of tears is in his eyes.) Biplab was an influential leader. As per his direction, we get our workers united. At last…these brokers have murdered him by plotting a secret conspiracy. Again, you have come to arrest us. Wonderful governance! Wonderful country! Wonderful!

Police Officer	:	Shut up. I arrest you now. You will speak what you want to at the court.
Satyabrata	:	(Firmly) Today, we are punished without any fault/crime. Well, one day you will see, the factory will be ruined or toppled down at the distressed cry of people experiencing poverty.
Dharmapal	:	I leave now. Because of false allegations, we may be either sentenced to death or jailed. But we can never deny the time's pulsation. Time can overpower anything and anybody in the world. A new age will undoubtedly come. There will be the need of bloody revolution. Yes, bloody revolution!

[The Constable drags them to the Police Station.]

Andhalochan	:	Hah…hah…For ages like this, the revolutionaries carry on slogans. Let's go, Manager and my bosom colleague, Chaturasen! Now we have got time to rest. Yes, (Towards Police Officer) did you receive your new vehicle? If you need anything in future, you will tell me without any hesitation or shame. One more point to you, Manager Babu! Take severe action against the workers who take part in the strike. Suspend them. Hah…hah…hah…survival of the fittest.

[The light is off. The laughter is heard until the stage light is on. The Stage Manager again stands in the middle of the stage.]

Stage Manager : (Taking a long breath for the audience) Yes, what you have seen! The soul of Kansa is everywhere. Do you experience this at some levels of society or the institutes? The Kansa, who has taken birth from the human civilization, has not left anyone from his clutch. Different governance systems, different ideologies etc, can't destroy this soul of Kansa. Kansa has devoured all sense of values. I take a leave now, Sir! Can the eternal conflict of Krishna with the soul of Kansa and the play composed out of that end here so quickly? We are sorry that we are unable to give you any satisfactory conclusion. So, it's the humble request to you all, having seen the play, you can think of the way you can destroy Kansa's soul. Well, I leave now. I will never disturb you.

[After the Stage Manager leaves the stage, the laughter of Kansa comes in first. Then Kansa enters.]

Kansa : Hah...Hah...Hah...I am spread everywhere. I want to devour everything. I have enough hunger. I am immortal. Hah...hah...hah...Having disobeyed a hundred Krishnas, Ramas, Parshurams, the trajectory of history, and the evolution of time, I am marching ahead. I am Kansa, irresistible, violent, invincible... hah...hah...hah...
Light off
END

KOKUA

ABOUT THE PLAY

[After the screen gets removed, the message is announced.]

The *'Kokua'* anecdote, as enshrined in Sarala Das's Odia *Mahabharat* (Musali Parba) is a symbolic representation of doubt, disbelief, murder and terror that were commonly perceived in socio-cultural milieu of that era. That is also relevant in the contemporary period. Every one of us seems to be thrown into the bleak atmosphere of fear and terror in our vast social system. On the whole, the values of higher order, eagerness of the human heart, and the hopes are pushed into the open-mouth of *Kokua*. Everywhere is seen an atmosphere of terror and discomfort. The villages are destroyed, and the human values and attributes are distorted. Money, power and animalistic urge primarily capture the human mind. The idyllic hearts of the villages are torn apart by the wild wings of *Kokua*. Everything is destroyed: river, spring, land, forest, and the simple lifestyle of tribes. Displacement has brought a new problem to their life. There is no escape of the tribal village Dhamaguda from its clutch. The black cloud of terror is also spilled over this place. In this village, Shyamananda has built up an *ashram* and tries hard to change the character of the people here. Subsequently, he starts propagating the sermons of generosity and humanity. But his ideals of life do not hold good. In the end, Shyamananda, who opined one day that murder, destruction and terror are the yardsticks of social reformation, is defeated. For this, there is a need for changes in our hearts. Again, as was earlier, in the society runs the rule of *Kokua*. Shyamananda's fall is a temporary exhaustion or a communiqué of a different time that may be answered in the play *Kokua*.

PREFACE

I had conceived the ideas of play *Kokua* in 2010. Before that, I had visited for a decade the factories, industries and marked infiltration of capitalism in the tribal lands that were mostly affected by the Naxals. When we open the newspaper or hear the news of radio or television, we consistently get to know about the barbarous activities of the Maoists. The face-off between the Police and the Maoists, the report pertaining to the heinous war between the two and the dreadful consequences have disturbed the ordinary people's life. The lifestyle of the people gets imbalanced and changed drastically. The heavenly beauty of the simple tribal land disappears. The polluted air unleashed from the industrial set-up is poisoned and discoloured. The spring water, deep forest and the mind of the people become dirty and stinky in texture.

Everywhere is senced horror and terror. Everywhere, the clarion of war is heard. Humanity is lost. It seems to us that someone cries in the forest land. She is, perhaps, Mother Earth. In the deep forest is heard the sound of bullets, grenades, landmines, and explosion. The babbling brooks and the chirping birds, in the forest have left no indelible traces. Man himself has created this 'sphere of terror and menace' around him. In this context, the *Kokua* myth of the Sarala *Mahabharat* invites a new, but different era. Kokua here underscores the symbolic representation of community life and mass psychology that is imbued with fear, doubt, disbelief, murder and terror. The claws of *Kokua* and its wild wings clasp our surroundings firmly. Everywhere, starting from the rural to the most boisterous city life is spread its well-sharpened and poisonous nail, tooth, wing, and face. It has its ever-burning eyes. It has engulfed every sense of value. It has an irresistible hunger and never-ending violence.

The extreme development of capitalism has invited this *Kokua*. 'Dhamaguda' village, described in the play is also trapped in its clutch. The serene and sublime ambience of the village gets annihilated. Spring, forest and land are destroyed ruthlessly. Here, displacement brings forth another problem in the life. The black cloud of terror covers the surroundings. Having built up an *ashram* in Dhamaguda, Shyamananda tries his best to transform the character of human beings settled here. To serve the people experiencing poverty and the orphans, to bring back normalcy in the environment, and to restore the Maoists, engrossed in terrorism and complete annihilation, into the mainstream of society, he is determined to convince to bear the torch. Shyamananda says, "There is no need for terror, murder and destruction for social transformation. We should practise love, affection and generosity instead." He blows the clarion call first for changing the heart. At last he is defeated.

Then, in his fall and self-agony are still the hints of hope, light, and possibility. When the play ends, Dama says, "Oh.. (He goes to Shibu after Ajay) Shibu…Shibu…no…

no...no...why will this be our Shibu? This may be someone else. One who said, jungle will be of the tribes, land will be of the tribal communities, ... the brooks will murmur again,... he...how can he leave the world so early?...this is the work of Kokua...Our Shibu will kill Kokua...he will kill Kokua one day...yes...yes. "

With this flavour of myth, I have considered a tribal village as my background to unfold the issues of the Naxalite movement, the complexities of displacement and, after all, and the crisis of our national life. It is imagined in 2010. The secretary of 'Vartika' magazine and my bosom friend Dr Naba Kishore Dash published this play in its very first issue in 2012. I am grateful to him for this. After that, the play was staged successfully at different places in Odisha. Out of them, the play's staging by the well-known theatre group 'Trinetra' will be remembered forever. It was staged by the same theatre group at Rabindra Mandap on 04.07.2013, at the Kala Bikash Kendra, Cuttack on 25.09.2013, and for the All India Multilingual Play competition on 20.04.2014 at Panchpattamali Drama Festival, Damonjodi. Mr. Om Prakash Behera, was the director for all three successful staging of the play. This play was also staged by the 'Media Cultural Academy', Nachuni, at the Global Theatre Festival 2015, organized in Cuttack under the direction of Mr. Bhikari Charan Pradhan. On 13.01.2017, under the leadership of the director Purnachandra Samantray, the play was staged on behalf of the Balugaon College Dramatic Society. From this point of view, I am really indebted to all the actors, actresses and directors. At last, I say my Pranam to Lord Jagannath and dedicate this work of art at his feet forever.

Bijoy Kumar Satapathy

DRAMATIS PERSONAE

Dama
Ajay
Shyamananda
Bhola
Bidei
Atanu
Shiba
Goutian
Monika

PLAY

[*A musical note of terror and menace is played on the instruments. After the curtain gets raised, the movement of lights and the dances of black shadows are shown on stage. Dama hurriedly enters and stops at the middle of stage. He has lost his mental state because of some untoward mishap in his life.*]

Dama : (Laughing loudly) *Kokua*...ha...ha...ha...it won't leave anybody. It will ruin everybody...it will tear apart...it will swallow the gory bodies one by one. Everywhere is spread its claws. Its eyes are fireballs. It's marching ahead irresistibly with vibrated tongue. The hundreds...thousands...lakhs of *Kokuas* can come from the mouth of one *Kokua*. They are all stepping forward heavily. Let's go. Let's go. Oh, I see! It's here. Can't you see? Can't you see *Kokua*? Can't you hear its screaming? It is in every man's mind and body. The *Eraka* Forest! The *Jaduvamsha* (Dynasty of Yadavs) will be destroyed. Let's return...

	Lets all return. Kokua will engulf. The Darkness drops under the wild wings of *Kokua* (An imaginary frightful creature). The brooks are dried up. The *Sal* forests are burned. The forest dwellers vomit blood. The tribal huts are completely ruined. (Crying) Poison, poison is diffused everywhere. Deluge...the great deluge. Return...You all return...*Kokua* is marching ahead with long steps. (Dama becomes senseless while saying. From a distance, Atanu's voice is heard.)
Atanu	: Commando! Ambush the Naxal Camp from all directions. You see thoroughly that none of them escapes. Be ready, start firing. (The serene mid-night gets disturbed. The environment becomes chaotic for sometimes with severe outcry, with the sound of firing, the siren of vehicles and the sounds of police boots.)

(In the mean while the stage is lit. Here is a courtyard of an ashram. In the courtyard are seen a chair and two or three tables. In front of the yard is a raised platform with a Tulsi (Basil) plant on its top and smeared with cow dung, and the walls are painted. A door screen separates the courtyard from the verandah outside. The sound of firing is heard from a nearby place and then a young man groans. The bullet is shot at the leg of that young man, and it's bleeding profusely. From the gloves, masks, and the helmet it is marked that he gets wounded in a battle with the opponents. His name is Ajay. Out of severe pain, dragging his wounded leg for a while, he falls asleep at the courtyard before chaura (a raised

platform with a basil plant on its top). He is unable to move ahead. Having been there, he calls somebody with his distressesful tone.)

Ajay : Who's there? ...oh...it's very painful. Ah...water...hear...who is there... aha... (When there is no voice inside the house, he wants to fire the pistol out of anger. But the pistol doesn't work, as it's without bullets. Then he has thrown that pistol there. Thereafter, he shouts loudly after throwing the helmet.) Why don't you respond to me, staying at your home? Oh...listen to me! (Struggling in pain he removes both his shirt and baniyan and binds a portion of the baniyan over the wounds of his leg. Shyamananda comes out to the courtyard, sliding the screen raised at the door. Having seen the young man, he abruptly stops and nearing him, he asks the man surprisingly.)

Shyamananda : What's this? How are you here... your whole body bleeds...as if you bathed in blood...(After groping the young man's body, he looks at the wounded spot in his leg.) ...this is, perhaps, a firing at your leg. (Being confused)...severe bleeding...

Ajay : They have fired me uncontrollably. Our camp is exploded. I don't know how many of our comrades live. When I tried to jump this boundary, their firing was shot at my legs. Ah...water...

Shyamananda : Moni...Moni...

Monika	:	(Staying inside) Yes, Baba!
Shyamananda	:	Bring a glass of water and a mug!
Monika	:	Yes, I am coming.
Shyamananda	:	Yes, you will also bring the First Aid Box, while coming.
Monika	:	(Staying inside) Yes, Baba!
Shyamananda	:	Yes, for some days, the whole atmosphere is disturbed. In the forest, an eerie atmosphere of doubt and terror pervades consistently. The land trembles with the sounds of guns and grenades here intermittently. The blood drops are on the ground. Why? Why are all these?
Ajay	:	(groaning with pain) The Police have started the operation. They are furious (out of anger - loudly) we...we won't leave...annihilation...death...destruction...Ah...I...I will take revenge for this rightly.
Shyamananda	:	(Not allowing him to tell anything more) No, no,...don't say so. A destructive approach will completely ruin the entire social life. Who will benefit from this? Leave it... stop that story for the time being. You take rest now. After your recovery...(By hook or by crook, he has brought the young man toward the chair in the courtyard. He allows him to sit on the ground, resting his head on the chair to get some comfort. He has removed all

	the shoes and socks. Sitting beside his leg, he has covered the wounds on his legs with his towels. At this time Moni comes out with a glass of water, a mug and the First Aid Box.)
Monika	: Baba…water…(Having seen the wounded young man, she shivers.)
Shyamanand	: Yes, give me. (He helps Ajay drink water; affectionately he touches his forehead) What is your name, please? Where are you from?
Ajay	: (agitated) Why? What's the need? You will inform the Police. They will arrest me. Is it so?
Monika	: (getting afraid of the situation) Baba…
Shyamananda	: (Directing Moni to be silent with gesture and affectionately he speaks) No, no…don't think like that. This is an *ashram*. I am the manager. My name is Shyamananda. I serve the distressed and the poor. My daughter Monika helps me in this regard.
Ajay	: (Laughing) showing your sympathy for how many days…adjusting with the wounded society…hopeless…
Shyamananda	: (Anyway) All right. The medicines that I am with now can be used only for primary treatment after dressing. Tomorrow I will take you to Jeypore District Medical.

Ajay	:	(Shouting) No... I won't go there...
Shyamananda	:	(Smiling and in soft tone) Don't worry at all, my child! Whoever you may be? You have been hurt severely. You can stay here for the number of days you want. The *ashram* will take care of you. You will leave the place after you completely recover.
Ajay	:	I am Ajay Marandi.
Shyamananda	:	(with fear and surprise) Ajay!!
Monika	:	(with fear and surprise) Ajay!!
Ajay	:	Yes, the Naxal leader Ajay Marandi. The Government has declared two lakhs against my name. I am in the 'Most Wanted List' as prepared by the Police. People generally tremble having heard this name.
Shyamananda	:	(with the same kind of fear and surprise) Ajay...! (After the normalcy) Well,... whoever you may be...no problem. The motto of this *ashram* is to serve man.
Monika	:	But, Baba...?
Shyamananda	:	No need to fear, my daughter!
Monika	:	But, Baba...He is Ajay Marandi...
Shyamananda	:	(Laughing) Yes, the famous Mao leader who leads the tribal people of Odisha, Chhatisgarh, and Andhra Pradesh and tries to bring them together with the threat of terror and menace.

Ajay	:	Yes, yes...(groaning with anger) That naxal leader is Ajay Marandi. He believes in annihilation. The enemies who believe in classes will be destroyed. Otherwise suicide,...death. The tribes of the forest have already suffered a lot. They have lost their ancestral property. In the conspiracy of Government Officials and the capitalists the jungles are looted... How...how they will live... Aha...I know that the price fixed for my head is ten lakhs...get hold of me... (Shouting loudly) take me... to the brokers of the capitalists...the enemies of the motherland.
Shyamananda	:	(trying to make him understand) No Ajay, listen to me...Listen to my words.
Ajay	:	Take...Take me to the police station. Let me be imprisoned. But, Ajay Marandi before being caught...ha...ha...ha... (laughing like a lunatic, taking out a capsule of his pocket) Potassium Cyanide capsule...ha...ha...before being caught I will take this (He laughs wholeheartedly and becomes senseless there.)
Shyamananda	:	Ajay...Ajay...! (He embraced him.)
Monika	:	I am afraid of him, Baba...!
Shyamananda	:	You hold him a little, my daughter! We will help him sit there. (Both of them help him to sit.) He has lost his sense. He bleeds profusely. After bandaging

him, we will see what else can be done. Yes…(picking up the capsule lying on the ground) I will bury this under the ground. Otherwise, I will destroy it. Surprise…we are surprised by their arguments…the way they fire the people, similarly, if the situation so warrants, they also take their life at once without any hesitation. You hold him a bit…we will take him inside.

(At the time of taking Ajay into the room, the stage is lit off. In the mean time a Jeep's siren is heard. The police inspector has come to the stage and he is accompanied by his constable Bidei Samantray.)

Bidei : Maybe, the culprit is hiding somewhere here.

Atanu : Yes, here. We have shortage of time. On that side the combing operation is continued. We have to return to the headquarters soon.

Bidei : (Searching for the surroundings) Comb the area mindfully…the need of earnest inquiry… we will teach them a lesson… they can be rightly controlled.

Atanu : (agitated) Oh,…stand there. Mind it Constable Bidei Samantray. We don't have the order to enquire about the *ashram*. The ashram is associated with public sentiments. The administration may be humiliated by this. Do you understand?

Bidei	:	Sir…right…right sir… you are right.
Atanu	:	(Looking at the surroundings he speaks gently.) Well, Bidei, the small tribal village surrounding the ashram, on the brook bank, I cannot remember, what's the name?
Bidei	:	Name, Sir…Oh…Yes…Dhamaguda.
Atanu	:	Yes, you are right. It's Dhamaguda. Once there was our encounter, the naxal leader named Shiba Majhi died.
Bidei	:	We did arrest five of them, Sir. Without any bail, they are still working in jail. That's the most disturbing place, Sir. Be mindful.
Atanu	:	(Being serious abruptly) The people of Dhamaguda mustn't have forgotten Shiba Majhi. He was educated, and the friend of the public in need. Then, how is his name in the naxal list?
Bidei	:	Maybe,…that may be the tactics and conspiracy of the politicians.
Atanu	:	The people of the village, under the leadership of Shiba Majhi opposed the Ferro Alloys Plant. Their land will be captured and jungle will be ruined, that's why…
Bidei	:	Will; was there any other way out, Sir? Was the factory set up? Was it closed? The owner of the factory became rich along with the M.L.A. Harekrushna

	Gountia. They are all well-connected with the Government Officials. They get support from them. What can the tribal people do?
Atanu	: Well, Bidei, they can do what a tiger or a lion of the forest generally does, once they raise their voice. It seems to me that Shiba Majhi was good and healthy. Some people say, "He was not dead in the encounter." He runs from the Organization secretly. I don't know whether he is dead or alive. Well, you may leave now, Bidei.
Bidei	: (Hesitantly) …Sir.
Atanu	: (Angrily) It won't work, if you behave like that. You move to the village with this vehicle. I am going in another direction. Yes, are you with the phone number of Anti-Bombing Squad? In case of any emergency, you will call either to me or to them. Be quick.
Bidei	: Yes, Sir… (Bidei leaves. Atanu is absent-minded and walks unsteadily for a while. He speaks indistinctly Shiba Majhi…Shiba Majhi…Dama Majhi comes out of his house. He is half-mad. Pointing his fingers at Atanu, Dama laughs irresistibly. Astonished Atanu raises his pistol up.)
Atanu	: Hands up…
Dama	: (Laughing loudly) Kill me…shot the

bullet at me...kill me...what will Dam Majhi get, if he is alive? Half of the people of this slum have already gone somewhere in search of life. Everything is calm and quiet here for the last three to four years. There is no celebration of *Puspuni* and *Karama* Festival in the village. The factory is to be set up. Let our land be lost, let our forest be lost, let the people die... let factory be set up... ha...ha...ha... factory is being set up at the cost of our land. Everywhere, the poison spreads. Fear...see, they roam... swords are in their hands...they will kill...they will kill.

Atanu : Shut up, I don't have time to hear the useless story. Answer me what I ask you.

Dama : (Avoiding Atanu's question he convinces himself.) He left saying everything will be right. Our rights will be for the trees of the forest and the water of the fountains. All factories will be set up elsewhere. If we lose our land, how will we live? We will die out of hunger. (Eagerly changing the flow of conversation) Have you seen him? Has our Shibu told you when he will come back?

Atanu : That day he was shot dead in the police encounter...

Dama : No, Whoever is asked, the same response I have heard. You are also saying the same.

Atanu	:	Yes, all are saying what I say...then, that's right.
Dama	:	No, no, these are all lies. My Shibu won't die like this. (Moving to different directions he tries to hear) Oh, he is here! He is saying me from some other place...yes, he is saying...he is saying to all the people of Dhamaguda...(Shibu's voice echoes in air- no, no... who is to be afraid of...who have we to fear? We are the tribal children of the forest land. Neither have we borrowed from anybody, nor have we consumed of anybody's? They have looted all from us. We don't have land, we don't have forest, and we don't have a handful of rice. When we raise our voice against injustice,...the threat of killing with barbarism...Shiba Majhi is not afraid of death...He is invincible...yes, yes, he is invincible.) Have you heard... have you heard, Babu...Have you heard what my Shibu says?
Atanu	:	Oh...this is entirely useless!
Dama	:	Fear...fear of Kokua...ha...ha...ha... this type of terror would have not been perceived earlier in the forest, if the tiger had maddened. Now-a-days,... the blood-thirsty people are ruling. The forest land asks for blood...gory

of blood...ha...ha...ha...you need the factory...let the tribal land be lost... what do you think?

[Shyamananda comes.]

Shyamananda : What are you saying, Dama? (Atanu says pranam to Shyamananda. Because of absent-mindedness his face is full of displeasure.)

Dama : *Kokua*...Have you seen *Kokua, Mastre* (a word of respect used to address a teacher)? It has big eyes...hundreds of eyes...hundreds of legs...two wings like vast mountains...its tongue ever-vibrating...(hinting at Atanu) these... these people have brought the *Kokua... Mastre*...let's walk to kill *Kokua*... otherwise *Kokua* will swallow all of us. Come, *Mastre*...(He tells all this while embracing Shyamananda completely.)

Shyamananda : (Trying to convince him) You leave the place, Dama...Take rest...Doctor has instructed you not to speak anything unnecessarily...Come with me.

Dama : Only our Shibu will kill Kokua. The tribes will get their forest back, their land back; *Sal* trees will blossom...the brooks will babble with more crystal clear water than earlier. Pure water will flow everywhere...yes, pure water. (Shyamananda has not allowed him to say more and taken him inside.)

Shyamananda : Come, Atanu. After a long time we are meeting again.

Atanu : (He is agitated, though not absent-minded.) Yes, Sir. Nearly ten years. I get appointed at the police station, after my training. Thereafter, I have been transferred to three or four places. Then I reached here one year earlier. Because of my workload, I can't meet you. Please, pardon me, Sir.

Shyamananda : No, no, why do you think of that? You have remembered me; that's enough.

Atanu : What I am now is only because of you, Sir. I was an orphan in those days. You have nurtured and helped me grow as Atanu. Had I not received your cooperation, how would I become a man (well-established in society) now?

Shyamananda : I was only a means. All this was the will of God, the Almighty. Apart from that, after the sad demise of your parents, had the priest of your village not brought you to our school, how would the relationship between you and me have strengthened? No need to be worried, though we meet after a long gap. Are we linked by our heart? Do you understand?

Atanu : Though we stay at a distance, I often ask about you. I have heard how you have been driven away from the

		school without any reason. After that, having reached here, you have built up the *ashram* here to serve and help the distressed and the downtrodden.
Shyamananda	:	(Taking a long breath) Yes, they had a complaint that this Shyamananda was making the tribal children revolutionary in their approach. He didn't teach textbooks prescribed for the schools; he is, instead, teaching Marxism…Maoism. Subsequently, on the pretext of this complaint, I had been expelled from the school. Then, what would I do after that? I am also a bachelor. I don't have family. My family means all the poor of the region…the tribal children.
Atanu	:	(with tearful eyes) Sir.
Shyamananda	:	Considering me as my model I will spend the rest of my life. But, it's very difficult, Atanu…To make one model alive…living with the values of life…Till this day I haven't compromised with anything. I move on like this.
Atanu	:	But, I couldn't keep up your words. I have been ungrateful to you. For that only I don't dare to stand before you. I have been forced to come to you on Government Duty.
Shyamananda	:	Duty…what sort of duty do you have at this *Ashram*, Atanu?
Atanu	:	Last night the Area Commander of the

	Naxals narrowly escaped with tricks, when there was combing operation by the Police here. Of course, from the Naxal camp, a lot of bullets, guns, grenades, and the rocket launchers were seized. These have been brought from China through Nepal. The C.R.P.F. General Major Sukhvinder Singh was the head chief of the operation. I was an assistant to him. (Taking out a postcard size photograph of the pocket) This... This is the naxal leader Ajay Marandi who escaped.
Shyamananda :	Oh...then this is the person...(He behaved as if he didn't know.) Well, you are searching for him. Aren't you?
Atanu :	Yes, Sir...if he is caught alive or dead; the person who will do this, will be rewarded ten lakhs as per the announcement of Police Headquarters to the media.
Shyamananda :	Then, how is our *ashram* linked to that matter?
Atanu :	(Keeping the photo in pocket) It is reported that he is hiding himself somewhere in this *ashram*.
Shyamananda :	So, will you do the search operation here at the ashram? You...do you suspect me?
Atanu :	No, Sir...no...this may be the hypothesis of headquarters. But, there are the traces of crawling outside your ashram's

	boundary, and blood drops are spotted on the ground. The Dog Squad has also indicated the same. The culprit must hide himself somewhere here. Then I will enquire about the ashram with the help of dog squad. ..My conscience obstructs me…I come, we meet each other, this is enough.
Shyamananda :	How do you believe me without any inquiry?
Atanu :	I couldn't keep up my words that day. What you wanted could not happen. I hurt you and Monica…there was no other way…Today I think, it's better to serve people experiencing poverty, staying at this ashram, than to work as an orderly of another officer.
Shyamananda :	(Breathing long) Atanu! Forget, what had happened earlier. Otherwise, you won't be happy. I have also told Monika the same story. I wish you and Monica would marry each other for a new life. Leave that…that didn't happen. Yes, I have heard that you are…
Atanu :	Yes…I married two years back…But, there is no peace in my life. My father-in-law bought me with money. I was poor. Money and wealth, however, tainted my cupidity…But the girl I married is very stubborn. My life gets shattered.
Shyamananda :	Atanu…

Atanu	:	(In mournful voice) Leave it, Sir, let me go.
Shyamananda	:	No. no…how will you leave? Please be seated, you have come here after a long time. Though I have discussed with you so long, I have forgotten to serve you a cup of tea. Moni…Moni…(He enters the room calling her, and Atanu obstructs saying 'no sir, no sir'. After a while Monica comes in with a cup of tea.)
Monica	:	Tea…I have brought this tea for you.
Atanu	:	(Distressed Atanu gets shocked, taking a turn and having seen Monica) Mo…ni…ka (The past has brought into his mind many bites of disappointment.) No…hold on…hold on, Monika…No need of it.
Monika	:	You have come here after a long time. You will leave without taking tea.
Atanu	:	I thought of leaving without meeting you…
Monika	:	It would have been better according to you. But, why? Believe me; I will never blame the past. You take this into account that we have never met each other anywhere. You are my guest and I have brought this cup of tea as per my father's words.
Atanu	:	To burn memories is to earn pains. It's tough to forget the past. I am not a

		stranger to you. You are using the word *apana*...(for 'you' in respect)
Monika	:	There is no other way except accepting the reality.
Atanu	:	I can't, Monika...I can't...
Monika	:	Atanu...
Atanu	:	Yes Monika...yes...when my marital life gets ruined, you...you are mostly remembered...
Monika	:	(Atanu, at the time of holding Monika's hands) No Atanu, no...please...Past is passed...why is it repeated again? You are an officer, well-placed, and I am an unknown girl adopted in this ashram...a refugee Bengali girl.
Atanu	:	I was also helpless and an orphan. This *ashram* has changed my life.
Monika	:	Time is changed now, Atanu. You are happy in your own identity. For you, this ashram and this Monika...these are all valueless. You...you go now. However, you have come here for an inquiry. You haven't come here to meet either me or my father. (More rigorously than earlier) What will you enquire about? ...You...don't you know about the ashram? If you doubt, come...come with me, please.
Atanu	:	No, Monika, no. I have already intimated this to the headquarters, before I reach

	this ashram. Now, it won't be right for me to doubt the ashram.
Monika :	(Taking a long breath) then, now you can leave. Yes, you can leave. (She leaves the place abruptly.)
Atanu :	Monika...(Passionately Atanu looks at the path Monika moves on. The light gets dimmed slowly with a sorrowful musical note. At this time there is a campaign marching ahead of the road. The slogan is "Farmers and workers want to make life better; Factories and industries are the need of the hour. Farmers and workers want to make life better; Factories and industries are the need of the hour, Let the chariot of progress roll in our country." Looking at the campaign Shyamananda and Ajay enter.)
Ajay :	The petty supporters of the capitalists have arranged this procession. The M.L.A Harekrushna Gountia has taken the leadership...this person forces the tribal people to work as the indentured labourers, and encroaches the tribal land. He has received a good sum from the company. So, he wants the industries to be set up here only.
Shyamananda :	For the betterment of society we should not expect anything from these petty politicians who support Capitalism, Ajay. We are, already on the path of destruction and degeneration.

Ajay	:	The society will better that moment when the enemies of classes will be neutralized. The only way for this is annihilation.
Shyamananda	:	No…no…Ajay. As a result of this, there will be anarchy in society. Nothing can be solved following the path of murder, terror and explosion. We have to change the heart or character of people.
Ajay	:	Then…is it possible? How can we think of 'changing the heart' of people who strongly believe in class difference and the self-centric classes of society?
Shyamananda	:	(Laughing) Nothing is impossible, Ajay. Your stay at the ashram has already been some days. You must have marked the lifestyle of this place. Here we don't worship any God or Goddess. We serve to people only.
Ajay	:	Truly, for this ashram, I have a weakness. You…Monika…this ashram…and its surroundings…really so good.
Shyamananda	:	Yes, Ajay, I will rest peacefully, having handed over to you the management of this ashram and Monika.
Ajay	:	But,,,I have already told you the saga of my life-journey. I have been working in association with a very strong Revolutionary Organization. But, I am exhausted today and your consultation has shown me the right path.

Shyamananda	:	Ajay, you understand, only revolution, counter-revolution...these won't bring you any solution. Along with that there is the need of reorganization. The 'change of heart' is the greatest of all. You are educated. You must have marked that this earth have flooded with many ideologies, revolutions... the people have received many *mantras* (dicta) ...many theories...but, all these are useless and in vain, if an individual's character isn't changed. The sense of disparity stands as a boundary. In the name of religion, community and ideology, the people are here at loggerheads and in continuous strife, engrossed in bloodshed and murder and terror. My journey is to change the character of human beings. This is the need of the hour.
Ajay	:	If nobody accepts this principle?
Shyamananda	:	Well...We must stick to this principle only. We will make a revolution in our thoughts and consciousness.
Ajay	:	(With deep breathing) The Commander-in-Chief of our Unit has messaged me to leave this place and join the unit.
Shyamananda	:	What have you answered him?
Ajay	:	I have denied and told him that I won't join any Revolutionary Organization. I want to lead a peaceful life...Life...I

		want to free my life that is clouded with terror. (Dama enters. While laughing loudly, he says.)
Dama	:	Kokua...everywhere the terror of Kokua...everything will be ruined... blood of river...*Eraka* Forest...the end of *Dwapar Yuga* (Laughing, he speaks at one stretch, having seen Ajay) ...Oh... when have you come...yes...haven't I told you....Shibu will come one day... (Eagerly, he embraces Ajay.)...you see... This is our Shibu...(affectionately)... Shibu has come...Shibu has come (loudly speaking)...has he not told us... jungle will be ours...land will be ours... the dead brooks will be rejuvenated with water again...Shibu has come...Shibu has come...(Clasping Ajay happily, he dances.)
Shyamananda	:	(Convincing him)...Yes, Dama...Shibu has returned...(To Ajay)...This is your Shibu...(He has instructed Ajay to approve what Dama thinks of him.)
Dama	:	(Pampering Ajay's body and sitting nearby him) Won't everything be set right?...will we get back our land of seven generations (ancestral properties)? ...(Crying) With the Police Force, the factory owner had driven us from our village...our ancestral properties were ruined...They had seized our wealth... will we get back the same again...

		(holding Ajay, he speaks eagerly)…You say, Shibu…why don't you say?
Ajay	:	(At the situation, Ajay is unable to control and with his tearful eyes.) Yes…we will return our village…the jungle will be ours…the land will be ours…come…come inside…we will talk there…when we will return our home (Village)…we will talk about that…(He takes Dama inside, while Shyamananda says.)
Shyamananda	:	Listen to me, Ajay! Consulting Moni, you will give medicines to Dama in time. You will also consult Doctor Mohapatra about your medicines.
Ajay	:	Yes…(He takes Dama inside. Then Harekrushna Gountia reaches there. He is very shrewd by nature and the local representative of the public. He is accompanied by the Constable Bidei Samantara. Both of them have seen Dama Majhi and Ajay Marandi.)
Gountia	:	Namaskar…Namaskar, Shyama Babu… Today, after a long time I have come here…you understand…I was on a procession in this road. Having seen the signboard of the ashram, I desired to have a meeting with you.
Shyamananda	:	Well, …I am very happy at this moment. You are the local representative of the region. You have never visited this ashram earlier.

Gountia	:	(Making a twist of the discourse) Your ashram now remains under a cloud of suspicion, Shyamananda!
Shyamananda	:	(in clear tone) what…in your eyes or in the eyes of others.
Bidei	:	Maybe…the business of the place…the deeds…the scandals …
Shyamananda	:	Please, shut up, Bidei! I am talking to the honourable M. L. A. Gountia. Don't obstruct us.
Bidei	:	I am the bodyguard of honourable M. L. A…I have been ordered from the Police Station…Now it's my duty.
Gountia	:	Stop, Bidei…We won't get anything from this imposter.
Bidei	:	Maybe…we will lose our prestige…
Shyamananda	:	(Agitated) Gountia. You have crossed the limits. Who is here the imposter? Can I know whether I am or you are? Having won the election, you are now the representative of the people. I have not ruined the people. (With a very solemn voice)…Being the broker of capitalism, I have not invited the industrialists to come over here and set up industries and factories at the loss of forest, fountains, and the tribal villages. I am a common man. I serve to the poor with my limited energy. I don't expect anything from anybody. Tell me whether you are or I am the imposter.

Bidei	:	Service…You mean service…Gountia Sir also serves to the destitute…Nobody comes to my mind other than him. I am unable to trace, when you have started serving to the people.
Gountia	:	(Being agitated) Shyamananda…Your ashram is the hotspot of all kinds of scandals and corruptions. You are talking of 'service'.
Shyamananda	:	The Earth has already tolerated the *shaitan* and *pichash* (an evil and barbarous spirit) like you.
Bidei	:	Yes…yes…This is enough.
Gountia	:	The shell of hypocrisy you have worn will be unsealed soon. The Special Branch has already submitted the report. Your ashram is the Training Centre of the Naxals. How can I disbelieve what I have seen in my eyes, Shyamananda?
Bidei	:	How?
Shyamananda	:	What do you want to say?
Gountia	:	Shibu Majhi…One who was a naxal got killed in the police encounter. His father Dama is not staying at your ashram… Tell Shyamananda…Have I told you a lie?
Shyamananda	:	Yes, after the death of his son,…after the company's encroachment of his land,…where would Dama stay without food and shelter? Where does my fault

		lie? Not only Dama, but also so many displaced people reside at this ashram. Whoever seeks help, gets sheltered at this ashram...he has worked for the ashram. In turn we have done the arrangement for his stay and food.
Bidei	:	Why do you allow the anti-governmental works?
Gountia	:	You are right, Constable Bidei. Shyamananda! There are many evidences against your anti-governmental activities. What do you think? You were the headmaster of one school. For being a Maoist you have been expelled from that place. I thought, "You will change yourself and be engaged in worshiping God, having built up an ashram here." But, what I see is entirely different. There is no change in your life. No changes at all.
Bidei	:	(Turning his face away from him) I also realize the same...There won't be any change in him.
Shyamananda	:	Have faith in me, Gountia...How will I help you understand? You are saying what I am not. You are my childhood friend...eventually you are now the politician...Now I am a common man...I am not controlled by either Maoism or Marxism. I have faith in human beings. My pride is for the entire humanity. Because of this, nothing is more true

	and eternal than human beings. I serve to that humanity...I have not committed any crime here.
Gountia :	(Laughing satirically) You are cheating... ha...ha...ha...
Bidei :	It seems to me, "You wear orange-coloured dress, but you are the most corrupted individual." Oh, my God! This is the ashram for the Naxals. (Looking at the surroundings) Bombs may be installed somewhere here. Landmines may be fixed...I will teach you a lesson...(He poses himself with the gun.)
Shyamananda :	(screaming) No...no...this is false... absolutely false...those who are forcefully evicted...in the tricks of the politicians like you...whose rice-plates have been thrown away...in the conspiracy of the officials who serve to you...what kind of crime have I committed, having served to them? How can I become anti-government? (Saying rapidly) Have you ever thought of the terror and bloodshed raised by the Maoists, Gountia? The root cause of their movement is poverty, indifference, displacement, and forgery of the civilized man. Time has come today...We have to transform them all with the bond of love and affection. Change yourself first. I think, you understand now, Gountia...

	Being a broker of capitalism, if you advocate on behalf of displacement, no solutions can be brought in.
Gountia	: Stop your all empty ideals and dialogues. You have been very talkative now.
Bidei	: It seems to me...Gandhi has returned.
Shyamananda	: Why do you criticize me? Return...He will return certainly one day...but with a new form...with an incarnation of the new age.
Gountia	: Shyamananda Babu! Don't waste time...I have a word (absorbed in thought) ...yes, that is ...you can give your statement...that can be the headlines in newspapers. In that we will be benefitted ...your...your ashram will get the grants of lakhs of rupees. Listen to me...your report will be that ...the agitation for displacement is unjust and illegal...the company focusing on its convenience will try to rehabilitate the displaced ones on priority basis. Based on their qualifications the people will be appointed in the factories. The ashram entirely agrees at the statements made by M.L.A. Gountia.
Shyamananda	: No...I can't report so.
Bidei	: Babu Shyamananda! Your vandalism won't work here.
Gountia	: (Angrily) Then, it's right. I will see you,

		Shyamananda! For how many days will you stay here at this ashram? Ajay Marandi is hiding at your ashram. The 'Most Wanted Maoist'...Tell me whether it's right or wrong?
Shyamananda	:	Gountia!
Gountia	:	He is the strongest leader of the Mao Organization raised up at Andhra-Odisha Border...the Area Commander.
Shyamananda	:	Yes, whoever he may be. I have not been hesitant to respect the humanity. I have helped the poor and the distressed. I have advocated the people to come out of their sphere of violence, bloodshed and terror...this principle our ashram has adopted since its very inception. (Twisting his speech) Yes...you are talking of Ajay Marandi. Having been severely hurt in the police encounter, he reached the ashram. I have helped him recover completely with my treatment. What has happened, then? Ajay has been completely transformed. Earlier Ajay was different from the present Ajay. He is joining the mainstream of society shortly.
Bidei	:	This seems to me...he may be somewhere here...we will save this parental soul, Sir...
Gountia	:	Listen to me, Shyamananda! Your ashram is the principal centre of the

	Naxalite Movement. Your person Bhola staying at the *ashram* will give information to the Police. He is now the police informer. Now he is in our trap… ha…ha…ha…
Bidei :	Maybe…Bombs, pistols, bullets and grenades are stored here…Bhola may report about this…Otherwise, he will be told to write down the same.
Gountia :	(With a sarcastic smile) when he has become an informer of the Police, he is our person. His son will certainly get a job in the company.
Bidei :	(Requesting) My son couldn't get a job though he passed the 10th Board examination in several attempts.
Gountia :	He will also get a job in the company.
Shyamananda :	This is a conspiracy…surely a well-plotted vicious circle…what's the reality? What are the rules and the sense of values? Our Dama rightly says, … KOKUAA…KO…KU…AA…KO… KU…AA…Nobody can escape from its clutch…(He laughs like a lunatic and cries subsequently.)
Bidei :	(Being jealous of) Hey (with fear in a raised voice he will speak)! KO… K.U… AA. (The light gets dimmed from the stage slowly. The musical note of terror and menace comes down gradually. Monika and Ajay are marked

		sitting together, when the light is lit on stage. Ajay gets fully recovered in the meantime.)
Ajay	:	(Getting up from the place) They ring me again and again, They also threaten me. They tell me to return and join their cadre ...Otherwise, the consequence will be very bad...the place where you are, how you are...we have bit by bit information about you. When I say them...my views...I have been changed, the solution of any problem is not violence and bloodshed...the answer I get back...changing the heart is an emotional state...We have to free ourselves from all kinds of emotions. That means we must sacrifice our feelings into the altar (the place to hold the sacrifice) of revolution.
Monika	:	I am terrified now, Ajay...Anything can happen anytime.
Ajay	:	Revolution...Counter-revolution... Conspiracy...strangely engulf the surroundings here. This is not the story of this place, Monika...of the whole country too. Fear...terror...disbelief... bloodshed...our social system is completely soaked in these words.
Monika	:	What will we do now?
Ajay	:	We will live with our philosophy and principles...

Monika	:	The dream that my father has seen…
Ajay	:	We will fulfill that. I have got a new life because of your love and care. This ashram has taught me a new mantra (principle) of life and shown me a source to live. I love you, Monika. I dream of you a lot, though I am fully severed from the society. You are, now the proof of my dream…That child will see this world soon…It will walk slowly with its little limbs…It will play in the grass field in front of this *ashram*.
Monika	:	We will sing the song of life, Ajay…the song of life to live.
Ajay	:	We will dance in the Puspuni Festival, and sing wholeheartedly in the Makar Festival…(From a distance, the musical tunings of song and dance can intoxicate anyone. When they have forgotten themselves, there is a phone call on their mobile. Taking the mobile from his pocket, Ajay says.) Hello…yes…yes, Comrade…No…I won't return… I have told you earlier…no…never…no…there is no need of my meeting with you… well…Thank you…(With exasperation while keeping the mobile inside the pocket, he says.) Sadashiba Rao again calls me…
Monika	:	Who is Sadashiba Rao?
Ajay	:	The Commander-in-Chief of Andhra-

		Odisha Naxal Organization. He has threatened me; I must return to the headquarters by the next week.
Monika	:	(Being worried) …Ajay…
Ajay	:	(Seriously) No…no…impossible…no question of my return…I know…to stay here and return again to this place for me is a question of life and death…Now I am strongly determined. (A chorus with musical notes is floated in the environment from the tribal village. Both of them stand up to dance rhythmically with the beats of drum, as this chorus touches their heart and soul.)
Monika	:	See, Ajay, how they are singing beatifully in the silvery night.
Ajay	:	(Anxiously) Yes, Monika. Joining the cadre for many days, I have forgotten the celebration of *the Makar Festival, the Puspuni Festival* and the dances and the songs. Today I am excited to dance…to sing…to enjoy life wholeheartedly. (Having heard the songs, Ajay's eyes are full of tears and he utters emotionally.) Can you hear?…Can you hear, Monika? They are expressing in songs…the Earth is below us, the sky is above us, and clear water flows in the brooks…saying *Juhar* (Namaskar) to you, God, the Almighty. Give us rain, give us crop…Bless us that no enemies will be ours. But what has

	happened today? Why does the social life run here unsystematically?
Monika	: Come...come Ajay! We will go there. In the nearby place there is the celebration of *Makar Festival*. Holding Ajay's hands she moves.
Ajay	: Let's go...(Both of them move fast to that spot. The director may play the tribal chorus song and dance on stage while Ajay and Monika join the group. With the drumbeats, the rhythms of music mesmerize the whole environment. The night gradually drops in. The waves of song and dance disappear. The sound of someone's jumping into the boundary is heard. In the darkness of night, "Who's there? Who's there? Who's there?" Shymananda calls them behind. A young man enters the stage, wearing a black dress and a mask with a pistol in his gloved hands. He comes secretly from an opposite direction where Shyamananda stands and points the gun at him instructing not to shout. Otherwise, I will fire you only.)
Shyamananda	: (Normally) Yes, you can kill me...I don't fear to die...This Shyammananda is not afraid of the gun's bullets and the sharp point of the bayonet...then...why are interested to kill me? (The stranger seems to be acquainted with the voice of Shyamananda and he tries to pull the

(pistol to the backside of his head. Taking a turn Shyamananda now looks at him without a blink and the man does look at him thoughtfully. The stranger opens his mask, and throws his cap and pistol. He looks at Shymananda with tearful eyes and a face overgrown with a beard. Later on taking the dust of his feet he cries loudly. Shyamananda is very anxious and calls him softly.)

Shyamananda : Shibu…Are you Shibu? …that clever sharp-witted guy of Dhamaguda village…(He embraces Shibu.)

Shibu : (He cries only and becomes silent while Shyamananda clasps him intimately. From his silence, it seems to him as if he were Shibu. After some time, he separates himself to a distance from Shyamananda, clearing his tears and allowing him to say.)

Shibu : No…Shibu Majhi is shot dead in the Police encounter…I…I am not Shibu…I am Sadashiba Rao…

Shyamananda : (Being shocked) Sadashiba Rao… Sadashiba, in the 'Most Wanted List' of the Police…

Shibu : Yes…I am that Sadashiba…

Shyamananda : No…no…this can't be…speak the truth to me, Shibu…The person who has helped you grow from a child to a young man…who has taught you to be man…

		how can you deny him? Are you telling him a lie?
Shibu	:	Sir...(eagerly) I have learnt from you...to speak the truth... telling a lie is committing a sin...I...I...your most affectionate, the most lovable Shibu of Dhamaguda village, Sir...I am not dead in the encounter...This was the trick of our Organization to divert the attention and determination of the Police Force towards us.
Shyamananda	:	(Overwhelmed in happiness) You are right. You have come. Ajay has reached here...Our ashram will smile. That you have come here is really good, Shibu... Dama...Dama...O, Dama! You hear! Shibu has come...your only son Shibu, mostly loved in the family...
Shibu	:	(Controlling his emotion and closing the mouth of Shyamananda) No... You won't express my true identity to anyone, Sir. Remember me that I am Sadashiba Rao...Shibu is shot dead in the police encounter many days ago. So, Sadashiba Rao's identity is for me and our Organization...that is good for all of us. Sir, please remember that Shibu has never returned or he won't return in future. The Commander-in-Chief of the Naxal Oganization, Sadashiba Rao, has come to take Ajay Marandi with him. My ten or fifteen comrades are waiting outside...

Shyamananda	:	Shibu…
Shibu	:	Yes, Sir…I live in a tunnel of darkness. There is no possibility of my come back. You will tell Ajay that I have come…and to my *Baa* (father) whom you take care of him very earnestly at this ashram… you will tell him too…(eagerly in loud voice)…You have met Shibu…He has told…He doesn't know when 'good time' will come…when the jungle will be ours…when the brooks will babble… He doesn't know…He doesn't know at all…(Saying this he cries profusely and steps out of the place hurriedly. Shyamananda stands still there with eyes full of tears. The stage is completely dark. A sorrowful music is played on. This musical note captivates the audience to sit silently for a while. When it comes to an end, there is marked a wild rampage outside. Subsequently, there are the siren of a Police Jeep and the sound of firing. The Police start announcing outside.)
Announcement:		Shyamananda! You, along with the most wanted naxal leader Ajay Marandi and others, surrender before the Police. If you don't surrender, the Police will enter the *ashram* premises forcefully. If there is any obstruction, there will be bloodshed. You will be responsible for that. (On the stage is heard the musical

notes of fear and terror. Then, there is the cry of Monika's labour pain. Ajay (who is inside the *ashram*) is now unsteady and disturbed. The siren of police Jeep and the sound of police boots disrupt the serene atmosphere of the *ashram*. Ajay looks at different directions carefully and again comes back.)

Ajay : No…The police have gheraoed the ashram…No question of taking Monika to the hospital…(Atanu comes hurriedly and raises pistol up to Ajay.)

Atanu : Police Operation is started now, Ajay. Now you are under arrest. If you try to escape from this place, I will fire you. (From the other direction Shibu, in the name of Sadashiba comes. He is masked with a pistol in his hand. He also points his pistol at Ajay.)

Shibu : (Shouting) No…I will take Ajay Marandi with me. He is of our cadre. He will return to our camp.

Atanu : No! Impossible! He will be under our custody. (The cry of Monika's labour pain is clearly heard.)

Ajay : (Disturbed) Monika! Moni! (to both of them)…me…leave me (He prepares himself to leave.)

Shiba : (Raising the pistol) Ajay…if you move one step ahead, you will be smashed.

Atanu	:	(Shouting) Both of you are the police target, Ajay Marandi and Sadashiba Rao...(Both of them are shown the pistols in both the hands and comes closer to them slowly.) You have time... Surrender yourselves to the Police...
Shiba	:	Listen to me, Police Inspector, Atanu. By any means Ajay Marandi will return to our camp. See...(He shows Atanu a Remote Control.) Throughout the ashram are fixed the landmines. Dangerous bombs and explosives are set in the surroundings. The Remote Control is in my hand....ha...ha...Ajay...come to me without any hesitation. Otherwise, the ashram will explode and completely ruin...Monika's body will be scattered into pieces...(sarcastically) your future heir too. (laughing) there will be no trace of your future generation.
Ajay	:	Shibu...
Shibu	:	No...This is not Shibu...I am the Area Commander Sadashiba Rao...This is his instruction.
Ajay	:	(in breaking voice) Sadashiba... Sadashiba Rao...You...You are my childhood friend...Shibu...
Shibu	:	the useless story...I have forgotten all my childhood days...my father...my mother...Dhamaguda village...There is only one truth...Annihilation...

	Neutralization…Devastation.
Atanu	: Oh, I see!…You have gone to this extent. Haven't you?
Shiba	: (Sarcastically with the raised voice) Destruction…Annihilation…Nobody can save you…
Ajay	: (more disturbed than earlier) Won't you all allow me to lead my life peacefully? A person like me searching for a way to live won't be allowed to breathe silently here. You say, Sadashiba Rao…you say the Police Inspector, Atanu…. you say, please? Please, let me live. (Mournfully)
Atanu	: (With raised voice) Surrender yourself to the Police first, Ajay. Then, after that…
Shiba	: Come back to our Camp, Ajay…They are waiting for your presence…
Ajay	: No…Never…
Shiba	: Ajay…
Ajay	: (Twisting the conversation) well… Yes…I…then, I will go…I will go certainly…(When Shibu is happy with these words, taking turn immediately, Atanu fires a shot at Shibu and Shibu falls down. The Remote Control is separated from him, when Atanu calls him loudly, pointing the pistol at him. On the other side, Monika's labour pain increases.)
Atanu	: (Calling Ajay) I say you to stand there,

		Ajay...Ajay...(He fires another shot at Ajay. Ajay falls down there.)
Ajay	:	(Groaning in pain) Ah...Ah...These... None of them allowed me to live, Monika...The simple normal life I led here is stopped permanently...ah...I...I will come back to you one day...to this Dhamaguda village...I will return... Monika...(He breathed his last there bloodstained.)
Atanu	:	Ajay...Ajay...(His body comes to rest permanently. Atanu realizes this. He sits beside the bloodstained dead body of Ajay. His mobile rings up, and he attends the call.) Yes, Sir...The dead bodies of those who are in our target are here, Sir...Yes, Sir...Ajay Marandi and Sadashiba Rao (Loudly) No, Sir...there is no need...inside the ashram... are so many poor and distressed people...the Force entering the ashram...no need of firing ...no, Sir...Shyamananda is not a terrorist...I know him very well, Sir... Oh, My God! I am right, Sir...Please, listen to me...(Monika experiences more labour pain. Thereafter, the first cry of the child born there is heard intermittently...along with that the sound of breaking the *ashram* and firing of bullets makes the environment more chaotic and distressful. Atanu walks unsteadily, while attending the phone

call.) Oh, I say, stop it...stop it...stop firing (But the firing and the breaking do not come to an end. The new born baby crying is held in one hand with clothes and brought closer to his chest and Shyamananda steps up the stage holding Monika on the other hand.)

Shyamananda : (Having seen Atanu) The ashram is completely ruined...come...come, Atanu...Arrest me...Arrest Monika... She is the wife of a terrorist...And this newborn baby...Arrest it too...(He cries like a mad person.)

Monika : Baba! ... Give me the child...let's leave the place...(Shyamananda hands over the child to Monika.)

Shyamananda : Where will we go, my daughter? Everywhere this Shyamananda is defeated...defeated...(He has seen the dead bodies of Ajay and Shibu.) Ajay... Ajay...Shibu...(He cries helplessly.)

Monika : (Sitting beside Ajay's dead body) Listen to me, Ajay!...Open your eyes...See once...This son is exactly like you...open your eyes, Ajay...Open your eyes... (When Monika and Shyamananda cry, Atanu comes to them like a culprit.)

Atanu : (To Shyamananda) I am undone, Sir! As directed, I have executed the order. (Shouting) Yes, Sir...I am a slave... My conscience and my humanity are sealed before my slavery. (The eyes are full of tears, and his tone now becomes very emotional with sadness.) I leave you now, Sir...What happened here was beyond my control...I don't know whether you will pardon me or not. I don't know whether I will meet you again...But today, I have sent my Resignation Letter to the Higher Authority...Yes...My conscience tells me...I will join and support the poor, the distressed, the starved and the displaced people...I will support the people who stir themselves in different issues...and I will work for them... (While he leaves the place hurriedly, Shyamananda says.)

Shyamananda : Terror...Fear...Menace...Disbelief...in the surroundings...the blood currents in the springs...the poison is diffused in the air...where is the hope to live? Where is the rhythm of healthy life? Where? Then...(coming closer to Monika and bringing the child back to his lap) this child...which path will the child follow in future? Love and affection or destruction or the path of terror...? Which path? (Dama comes hurriedly. He stops, having seen the two dead bodies and Monika and Shyamananda there. He sits down there. He flips the dead bodies. He can't stop his tears.)

Dama	:	*Mastre* (O Teacher with respect)...what are, all these, happening?
Shyamananda	:	Dama...Let's move fast...we don't have time...
Dama	:	(Moving to Ajay and then to Shibu) Shibu...Shibu...No...no, no...this is not Shibu...He must be somebody else. (Getting up from the ground) He told, "The forest will be of the tribal community...the lands will be of the tribal people...the brooks will murmur again (smiling)... How can he die... how can he desert us now...No...No... All these are the works of *Kokua*...Our Shibu will certainly kill *Kokua*. He will kill *Kokua*, certainly...Yes, he will... Yes..." (All of them cry loudly at last. Then in the atmosphere is heard the title song- "Darkness Drops in"...)

Lightoff

APPENDIX

Song No: 01

Two songs are incorporated with this play: The first one titled "Darkness Drops In, Deadly Time Roars Everywhere" is to be sung at the beginning and the other one in the end of the play by both the male and female singers. The second one will be rendered in chorus while the tribal people will dance together.

***Kokua*: An Imaginary Frightful Creature**

Darkness drops in,

Deadly Time roars everywhere,

When everything gets burned,

Heavily *Kokua* steps in.

Kokua, Kokua, Kokua,

Springs dry, trees die,

From the land, blood drips,

Thwarted everywhere, Love and Affection,

Heavily *Kokua* steps in.

Kokua, Kokua, Kokua,

Dreams shattered, smiles smothered,

Love blighted, and souls severed,

Merchant sucks the life-vein,

Heavily *Kokua* steps in,

Kokua, Kokua, Kokua.

Song No: 02

(While dancing, this chorus sung)

O Earth! Thou art our mother!

Thou art our mother!

Thou art worshipped for ages,

At each home of our village. (Refrain)

Babbling brooks and rivers stream,

A soothing breeze touches our limbs,

Our joyous mind climbs,

For whole day and night,

thou art our Protector. (Refrain)

END

Black Eagle Books

www.blackeaglebooks.org
info@blackeaglebooks.org

Black Eagle Books, an independent publisher, was founded as a nonprofit organization in April, 2019. It is our mission to connect and engage the Indian diaspora and the world at large with the best of works of world literature published on a collaborative platform, with special emphasis on foregrounding Contemporary Classics and New Writing.

www.ingramcontent.com/pod-product-compliance
Lightning Source LLC
Chambersburg PA
CBHW060615080526
44585CB00013B/843